God's Woman

In Her Own Destiny

Min. Parker,

Loving Thanks

Sharon Holliday

God's Woman

In Her Own Destiny

Sharon D. Holliday

ARMOUR OF LIGHT
PUBLISHING

Chapel Hill, North Carolina · Charleston, South Carolina

Published in the United States of America by
Beautiful Feat Press
an imprint of
Armour of Light Publishing
P.O. Box 778
Chapel Hill, North Carolina 27514

Visit us at: www.armouroflight.org

Design by Michael E. Evans

ISBN 978-0-9817120-7-9

Library of Congress Control Number: 2008939754

First Edition

10 9 8 7 6 5 4 3 2 *1*

NKJV Copyright © 1982 by Thomas Nelson, Inc.

NIV Copyright © 1973, 1978, 1984 by International Bible Society
Holy Bible. New Living Translation copyright © 1996, 2004 by Tyndale Charitable Trust. Used by permission of Tyndale House Publishers.

The Message Bible: Copyright © 1993, 1994, 1995, 1996, 2000, 2001, 2002 by Eugene H. Peterson

These dictionary topics are from
M.G. Easton M.A., D.D., Illustrated Bible Dictionary, Third Edition, published by Thomas Nelson, 1897. Public Domain, copy freely.

Holy Bible. New Living Translation copyright © 1996, 2004 by Tyndale Charitable Trust. Used by permission of Tyndale House Publishers.

Dedication

**To my husband, mother and father,
and sons, daughters and sisters, brothers
For all your love and inspiration.**

To every woman that has struggled with their identity in Christ because their past has a different image.
To every woman that has experienced failure of any kind.
To every woman that has experienced verbal and or physical abuse.
To every woman that missed the mark and feel they can't get up.
To every woman because she has been marked to be God's woman, accept Him.

~

He will show you how to be who He created you to be.
To all the young girls-to becoming God's Women

~

Lord, I pray that you help each woman to allow your peace to reign in them.
Cover them with confidence
And may their hearts embrace
God's Woman inside of them.

~

To the men...

I pray that you truly be men of God and love women as your sisters as Christ loves the church.

May you aid the women in your world to become God's Woman.

Foreword

Extraordinary Visionary Woman

Standing as any other ordinary woman
Looking out the window
Watching the beautiful autumn leaves
Being blown by the wind;
She's far beyond ordinary though
She's an extraordinary visionary
Watching heaven paint the earth
Listening to the whispers of Heaven
As it rejoices in satisfaction
  Creation's obedience
  Souls being touched
  Lives being changed
As knees are bowed in intercession
As the heaven releases it waters
She sees beyond the scattered water falls
Thirst being quenched
  As each creation sips its portion
  Of heavens pouring rivers
She's an extraordinary visionary
Watching heaven pour out its provisions.

And when rushing winds mix with stormy rains
As the sounds turns as anger
She's an extraordinary visionary
That listens
She hears the Savior speaking
And the storms shackled
By the spoken word "peace be still"
And peace calms the earth

She's an extraordinary visionary
That looks beyond
What is in plain view,
While undergoing the changes
That takes place in life and the trials of life

Though the storms are vivid
She's an extraordinary visionary
That sees Him reign
Raining the victory
As she patiently awaits the manifestations with joy
She is patient
Trusting
She's an extraordinary visionary
Woman that knows she belongs to Him
Knowing that He is carrying her through it all.

Table Of Contents

Dedication   5
Foreword   7
Introduction   11

Poetic Meditations (Part 1)   13

    Invigorating Praise   15
    Beautiful You   16
    Broken and Restored   17
    Woman   18
    Phenomenal   20
    Intimate Moments   25
    Woman   26

Poetic Meditations (Part 2)   31

    A Sweet Meditation   33
    Intimate Moments   34
    I Am Naked   35
    I Love Nothing More Than God   36
    Intimate Moments   38
    The Naked Life   39
    Don't Listen to the Devil   44
    Intimate Moments   52

Poetic Meditations (Part 3)   53

    Eve's Past, Our Future   55
    Life Lessons   56
    You are a Masterpiece   57
    My Garments Speak   58
    Sanctified Sanctuary   59
    Queens & Princesses   60

Aim to Please   **61**

Basic Essentials of God's Woman   **64**

Immoral Or Virtuous A Choice   **69**

Authentic Sisters   **74**

Poetic Meditations (Part 4)   **79**

God's Woman   **81**

Prized   **82**

Loving My Sister   **83**

I'm Not Perfect   **84**

Divine Attention! Domestic Formation   **86**

Another Life Lesson For Me   **93**

God's Woman Reaches Her Destiny   **95**

Let Go Of The Past   **98**

God's Woman   **100**

Poetic Meditations (Part 5)   **101**

Divinely Packaged   **103**

The Confession of God's Woman   **104**

Enjoy Life! Even the Simple Pleasures   **105**

About The Author   **113**

Order *God's Woman*   **115**

Introduction

"God's Woman" has been brewing in my spirit for years. Burning in my heart over the years were three questions; what is God's Woman? What is she all about? How does she become that? I guess if you want to understand something you need to go back to its origin, where it started. I thought about things, such as; what I really wanted in life and where I really want to end up in life.

As girls, I believe we've all had our dreams. They seemed like they could only happen in a great fairy tale. In our youthful innocence we pay little attention and do not understand the value of trials before triumph. Every girl's dream is possible in Him, because He gives us nothing that he can't bring to pass. It's up to us to allow Him to bring it to pass, by yielding our lives to Him.

In writing this book, I want to remind you that there is a Queen in you, live royally in Him, right where you are, to where He takes you. "Queens" are female members of a royal house. We, as women of God, are members and daughters of God, with power and authority to rule in the earth. Little do we know this, until we realize who we are and were created by God to be.

"Become the Queen you are to its full potential, teaching the little princesses to become Queens and follow them." In other words be the example, Woman of God, teach all the daughters who are in your world to grow up to be God's Woman.

As this so burned in my heart over the years, I asked myself these questions. "What is God's Woman?" What is she all about? How does she become that?

As this book unfolds in my spirit with indescribable expectancy we will see the creation of God's Woman.

Poetic Meditations
For
God's Woman

Part 1

Invigorating Praise

Here I am again
Dancing before
My King
The joy of my soul
Lifts me
No matter where
Life tries to take me.

My hands lifted high
Feet move'n
My body
Is in the groove
Of intimate praise
Unto Him alone.

My soul remembers well
He is greater than
Any situation
Any personal failure or frustration
I may experience.

When I am done
I see the consequences of my praise,
I am strengthened!
I want more!
I am above!
And
Not beneath life's circumstances!

In His presence,
I dance!

Invigorating
Praise!

Beautiful You

He created you
In your very own
Uniqueness
That no other is to be compared
For you have yours and each one
Has theirs.

Woman to woman
Of course, we must all understand
We add to one another,
Through
Knowledge and wisdom gained
As we strut down
Womanly lane.

Love is our stronghold
to make it
Beyond the she said,
Did you hear 'bout
So and so girl,

We take reign
Woman to woman on our knees
Showing God's love in
all our deeds.

No hidden agendas!
Women
Committed by love,
We gossip?
We choose, "Not!"
Ain't got
Time,
We're sisters
Woman to woman committed
To uplift,

We must open our eyes
and see this clear;

Satan
Comes to kill, steal and destroy
A sister loving a sister
A sister being a sistah.

That Love, Satan fears!

Woman to woman
Guard your heart,
And open your eyes and see this clear;
We have too much victory
To maintain,
His glory
To bring
With
No shame,
In Jesus Name.

We are beautiful,
We are unique,
Together we stand.

Whatever your dream,
Your mission
In life
Woman to woman
And sistah too
For one another, we must show,
I'm here for you.

Walk your path
As I walk mine
Faithfully and prayerfully so
With His destiny in mind
And remember
It's this kind of love that makes
You such,
A beautiful you!

Broken and Restored

Broken from
Painful things in her life
Abused and misused
Feeling worthless
Trying to measure up
Deep depression
From rejection
She's been broken.

Searching for life's
Voids to be
Filled
"There must be more"
She sobbed,
Realizing
Her life's been robbed.

Down the cheeks
Flow the tears
Her cry,
You heard.

~

Your word proclaimed.
Broken forth and restored

~

You reached in
Picking up this shattered
Broken life,

She now knows
She matters
She's loved.

Her hunger now satisfied,
Her voids now filled,
She has forgiven
And been forgiven
She knows she's precious in Your sight,
She's been broken but, now restored.

"Woman"

She walked with her hips
Swaying from side to side
And her head lifted
What a confident glide.

She wore a hat
That said
She was bold
As a lion
Though her spirit is like a gentle
dove.

Step'n in a room
With God as her head
She has no fear.
She's a woman that leads.

She is whimsical in her own way
In a class of her own
From the motherland
Of many
Within herself
She is each of us
She is not alone.

One of the fair, yet chocolate and
Smooth tone
Beauty
All in one,
Beautifully
Reflecting you, reflecting me.

No, she's not a slim
And perfectly fit
Swimsuit doll
But,
When you look at her
You can't help but think
What an exhibition of God's Excel-
lence in your sight

Outward beauty
She has!
That radiates

From her inward
Spirit,
All can see.

She's witty.
She's clever.
She fits in a room
Like a glove
on your hand
Without a word
She makes a stand.

When she speaks
Don't misunderstand.
She's sassy,
Yes, lively,
Quiet and wise,
Packaged well
A royal prize,
She's woman.

Her love for her children goes abroad
The womb of her heart
Births
Agape love,
Straight from the throne room
Out of the heart of our Father above.

We would say
In a term used today
"She's tight"
Bowing with grace
Humbly so
She's got style.

Her eyes glide across the room
And when she smiles
Sunny and bright
She ushers in heaven
all it's joy
Such sweet aroma
Must be God's
Beautiful perfume.

She is you and me
Oh boy!
Powerful in heavenly might,
She is woman

Uniquely designed
With purposed
And her mission
In mind.

Sister to Sistah
To one another
Fervently kind.

Each of us are
"Woman"
Royal Child of the King
Queen
Predestined by Him alone.

Look at her and see who you are by God's design
An extraordinary, rare, extra special,
Phenomenal being,
A diamond, a ruby too
All the jewels,
But,
Rare to find,
Her in you if you're not
Genuinely kind.

This example woman to you and me
Clearly we see,
What God wants
You
"Woman"
to be.

Phenomenal

Phenomenal is unique, extraordinary, rare, and extra special. It's a word that is personal to me in many ways. Phenomenality's what I've felt a long time. When it comes to describing my life, my love, myself, and most importantly my God, phenomenal is the word that fits and ranks high. Please don't misunderstand me; God is beyond description to me because He is God! Above All!

It was in the eighty's that I began my Christian walk. I had unusual experiences during the separation of old and familiar things. Before I committed my life to God I began to lose some social desires. I began to want to go to church instead of going out. As a matter of fact, I remember the last time a girlfriend of mine and I went out. I remember being on the dance floor and all of a sudden I could hear the music but it was fading away and I was moving and the people around me were too, but I was no longer there, in that setting, something was departing. I thought I might have had too much to drink.

"All I could think, when the music stopped, was it was time to go?" Something just wasn't right. What was happening to me? Something was drawing me in a different direction. "Phenomenal huh?"

Later after the invitation of some special people and truly and divinely orchestrated events in my life, I start attending church. After all, in my thinking, my children were growing up and I needed to give them something good that I was familiar with as a child, church. It was the prayers of the saints availing in my life and it was time for my life to begin. My real life and destiny were unfolding. Today I can't thank God enough for the change that my life has taken and the lives my life's change affected.

When I came in contact with this awesome all knowing, all present, and all-powerful God, a desire was deposited in my spirit that was beyond me. I knew something extraordinary was there but I did not know all of what it was or what to do with it. I had this incredible reassurance inside though. I yearned to know this God I committed to live for. Yea, I said life commitment. I was empty on the knowledge of God but full in desire.

When I gave my life to God I was told I was a new creature. Physically I didn't feel or see the new in myself. I only knew that I lost some old social desires but I still appeared the same. I did not have a revelation of 2 Corinthians 5:17-18 *"Therefore, if anyone is in Christ, he is a new creation; old things have passed away; behold all things have become new."* Although a change had taken place, all of who I was did not just go away instantly.

I had to undergo deliverance. I had test that were hard and test that I failed time and time again, but I never quit. I realize today that God created me a winner and winners do not comprehend quitting. Quitting is not in the equation of the Spirit filled life. That has lead me to where I am today. I understand that it was a process and in the process for my life and destiny it took the process to see God as I do today. The second part of that scripture says, *"Now all things are of God, who has reconciled us to Himself through Jesus Christ, and has given us the ministry of reconciliation."* This was something that became strong in my life too. I had some of the most unusual experiences with God and a lot of growing to do. That requires sitting at the feet of Jesus and learning of Him. I can honestly say today as I write this book, I have come to a point that I love nothing more than God.

In spite of the things I faced, I had this gigantic desire in my heart. This phenomenal desire in me was to be "God's Woman." Yea, God's Woman! That had to come from Him. It was part of me and who I would become--step by step. God created His woman, each with our own destiny. Maybe, that had been the inspiration, passion, and drive in my walk with Christ. I had this sense of belonging to God, having a Father that I desire to please. This desire is alive in me. Back then I could not comprehend it as I do today, I just knew it was there, but then did not mirror an image of God. I knew that everything that I saw wasn't what I wanted to end up being. God had better for me. From each of us God desires whom He created--YOU. He wanted who He destined to exist to reflect Him in the earth daily; which takes a relationship with Him.

I can clearly acknowledge that my life had been clouded by the lack of knowledge and lack of spiritual development because I had no relationship with God. I have learned to love and appreciate His loving kindness and His mercy toward me as His daughter.

Psalm 139:13-19 is a passage of scripture that has shaken my soul to know not only how wonderful God is but also what He thinks of me. It was a wakening of my spirit, soul, and body.

I'm coming to you today saying "Wake up! Wake up! And know that you are purposed by God."

Psalm 139:13-19

For You formed my inward parts;
You covered me in my mother's womb.
I will praise You, for I am fearfully and wonderfully made;
Marvelous are Your works,
And that my soul knows very well.
My frame was not hidden from You,
When I was made in secret,
And skillfully wrought in the lowest parts of the earth.
Your eyes saw my substance, being yet unformed.
And in Your book they all were written,
The days fashioned for me,
When as yet there were none of them.
How precious also are Your thoughts to me, O God!
How great is the sum of them!
If I should count them,
they would be more in number than the sand;

When I awake, I am still with You.

The Word of God expounds greatly and so beautifully about us. It lets us know how precious God thinks of us. We are His work. As a woman that has had children, I understand now, how important each day is, from the day that a child is conceived, born, and every day following. During my child bearing stages I was separated from God. I had no relationship with Him. Today though, I value His presence in my life and all that He does; as well as being able to depend on His faithfulness for anything. I value what he thinks of me. What more can I say? God cares for us. He also cares for all that matters to us.

When I came into the awareness of the gospel everything else in my life had failed. Things in the natural seemed fine, but I was miserable inside, without meaning or purpose. All the prior events of my life were not leading me to life until I acknowledged God. It was then that I began moving into an awareness of something greater. I finally found something to hold on to that would never let me go.

Read these scriptures with me: (NIV)

Deuteronomy 31:6
"Be strong and courageous.
Do not be afraid or terrified because of them,
for the LORD your God goes with you;
he will never leave you nor forsake you."

Deuteronomy 31:8
"The LORD himself goes before you and will be with you;
he will never leave you nor forsake you.
Do not be afraid; do not be discouraged."

The book of Deuteronomy itself is about a time in the lives of God's chosen people, the Hebrews. Moses, God's servant led them out of bondage from the Egyptians. They had gone through some unforgettable experiences. They rebelled and were unfaithful to God. They faced many things as they were heading for the promise land. And after Moses died, another man of God, Joshua led them faithfully.

God, in the book of Deuteronomy teaches us of His love and faithfulness toward His people. It let me know that I found someone that would never let me go, because who He is and His love for me.

I realize that this passion in me is a phenomenal desire to be God's Woman. I am confidently convinced it's important that you and I know who we are. You also need to know that it was God that created you. Woman, you were delicately created and only God could have designed such a beautiful creature as you. The image that He has of you is that of Him. Genesis 1:26 says *"Let Us make them in our image."* God made us unique, extraordinary, rare, and extra special. God made us phenomenally and we should develop a phenomenal desire for our very own destiny.

Intimate Moments

Read these Scriptures

Proverbs 31:10-31; Titus 2: 3-5; Review Psalm 139:13-19; 1Cor. 13

_____
_____
_____
_____
_____

Getting to Know You

Be real; take a moment to think about you right now. How do you see yourself? How are your relationships now with women outside of your closest relationships? Are there areas you need to work on to develop better relationships among our gender, woman to woman? How do you feel towards those who did you wrong?

_____
_____
_____
_____
_____
_____
_____
_____
_____
_____
_____
_____

Thought for Life
"God can always be seen through our love toward one another."

S.H.

Woman

I asked, "Where does God's woman begin?" And again found my-self in the book of beginnings. After reading Genesis I found that there are two places women exist. The first place that God's woman begins is in the supernatural realm--in the mind or plan of God. The second place that God's Woman begins is her physical existence, with God at creation in the Garden of Eden, on earth. This lets us know that we (women) are not an afterthought of God. If we had been an afterthought I don't think that God would have prepared a rib to be removed from the man at the appointed time.

Genesis 2:18
And the LORD God said, "It is not good that man should be alone; I will make him a helper comparable to him." NKJ

Genesis 2:20
Then the LORD God said, "It is not good for the man to be alone. I will make a helper who is just right for him." NLT

"But still there was no companion suitable for him."

We see that woman's beginning is with God; another important point here is that man and woman are made for each other in marriage. God did not establish alternative lifestyles.

Woman, God made this soft skinned human with delicate parts and formed her to be pleasing in every way to the man (male) of her unity. He clothed her with His Glory.

I can just imagine her feeling the warmth of God's presence and be-ing surrounded by His joys all at once as she opens her eyes to Him and hearing His voice, God's voice. This exemplifies a real need to keep God first and never stop spending time with Him.

And then, the man awakens and looks upon the woman, this beautiful creature of such beauty and poise. She hears her man's voice saying,

"This is now bone of my bones
and flesh of my flesh;
She shall be called Woman,
Because she was taken out of Man."

Notice something else here, the first words woman hears from man is acceptance. Ladies, stop letting men speak down on you. His words should be of love and acceptance. He should build you up and not tear you down.

Genesis 2:23
And they are united by God.

Genesis 2:23-24

and he brought her to the man.
The man said,
"This is now bone of my bones
and flesh of my flesh;
she shall be called woman,
for she was taken out of man."
For this reason a man will leave his father and mother and be
united to his wife, and they will become one flesh.

After Adam spent all this time on the earth attending the garden, naming the creatures, and having fellowship with God, his day for a wife had come.

When God brought her to him, Adam looked at her with love and acceptance, and told her "woman" you are the only one for me, you are a part of me, there is none before you "woman," except God. Isn't this beautiful how God set the order of marriage?

This should be the experience of every man that occurs when he meets the woman that will become "wife." I believe these very joys that Adam had at that moment is what God meant for men today. The only true way that you can identify her is first knowing and experiencing the love of God and then you will know if she is the right one. This also holds true to women knowing too; you do not need a premarital sample of each other.

Men rob themselves and you of something special when they become sexually intimate with you before marriage. God ordained this type of an intimacy for a purpose.

Genesis 2:24
For this reason a man will leave his father and mother and be united to his wife, and they will become one flesh.

Decide now for yourself that you are going to be ready for the man you desire as a woman of God. Woman you can be complete in your relationship with God as a single before you commit yourself to man. Here are some things for you to know along the way of dating and preparing for marriage.

First, stop looking for a husband. Prepare for one and he will find you. Men look for a good woman to marry. Just as Eve had time with God before she saw Adam, use your time with God to grow as God desires, loving Him and Him loving you; while you wait for Him to bring you to your man. Now this doesn't mean to physically sit in the house reading your Bible until he knocks at your door, but don't miss him if he does. Go about and enjoy life every day wherever you are. God's navigator is always working and can bring you to the right place at the right time. Trust God!

You also have to remember that Satan comes as an angel of light; meaning that some men use their instinct to prey on a woman when she's in a vulnerable period or experiencing low self-esteem, using his skill to deceive another daughter of the king, a queen that does not yet see her own worth for whatever reason; making her think that this one cares for me then giving in to becoming his hit and run victim. Leaving a wound that will either be cut open even more or healed because someone picked her up and carried her as Jesus does for us. As a minister, I know some parents and youth think I am old fashion because I still believe and teach the word without compromise to youth. I'm no kill joy and though my mother and village guardian of my day warned me, I have experienced the scars of lack of knowledge as well and knowing what life is like after having pre-marital sex and relationships that God did not ordain.

I speak truth concerning making choices of friends, music, dating, and alternative methods to drawing the youth to Christ. I may not draw but one, but I know that one is important to God because Jesus, as a Shepard, went after the one that was lost. I pray that the seed of the others will be watered by faithful mothers and fathers of the body of Christ that see all youth as their own and reach out to them to get them back on the path, not because of who they are or aren't, but because of the agape love of God that it takes to drive this and whom they really belong to.

When you are young you simply do not realize that he is not ready for a commitment, he's growing up. On the other side of the coin, I want to say there are good men out there. And more to be if they are guided by the word of God with examples for them as real men encouraging them to remain virgins. Letting them know that virginity is not a bad omen but its prognostic for a better future. *I detest the spirit that drives men to tell our young men to go out there and rape our young women of their future.* Yes, I said rape. *Her body does not belong to him. Un-marital sex is rape. You are taking something even with consent of the individual that is not yours. God did not give that to anyone but her spouse. I pray for our young men and old men to wake up and be godly men all the way.*

These types of relationship can take you through some excruciating side effects. Consider carefully your readiness to date and whom you date because dating requires maturity. You don't want to be taken on the ride and left behind on someone else's emotional roller coaster.

If you are one that has not been sexually active stay pure until marriage. Virginity is a gift that you can only give once in life. The next thing to know while dating and before you marry is how to identify a true man of God. He will never ask you to do anything outside of the Word of God. This means you need to know God, know His word as well as common sense right and wrong. He will encourage you in your walk with God always. He will also encourage the things that God has for your life. He will add to you, your value, and value you as a woman, God's woman. Your responsibility is to keep your standards on the level of God's word. Set godly standards in all things; dating, dress, work ethic, as an individual, and etc.

Now if you have not kept your virginity, repent. Turn away from that lifestyle and any people that don't want to live holy. Apply the things I said in the above paragraph and think of yourself as God does. Being a woman of God is still his plan for you. He loves you. Being God's woman is for you too. No matter what your sexual status is today; God's woman exists in Him.

I want you to realize; although the first woman, Eve sinned and placed us in a sin state by her disobedience, looking at the upside to the situation, we see how this experience shows us God's ultimate love for us in spite of her disobedience. This beautiful and wonderfully made creature that never knew the meaning of hurt, bitterness, grief, or envy allowed herself to talk to the devil in turn allowing him to inject seeds of deception, causing her to doubt God. Of course, it is easy to dismiss someone that changed the whole nature of what your life is supposed to be, but look at God. He was operating in that same love that created her even when He put them out of the garden. When He told them of the curse they had brought on themselves He revealed His redemption (Gen.3:15). So the upside of this is a loving Father that had a plan not to lose His children *if they begin with Him*. Everything begins with God and can grow to its full potential if God is at the head of it. God's Woman begins with God.

Poetic Meditations
Part 2

A Sweet Meditation

I think of you often.

I spent time with you today and I heard you say
 "I love you" in your own special way.
I think of you often in the course of the day
And I felt you with me every step of the way.

A friend asked me, "how I knew it was you" and I said,
"I know my Father's voice,
The voice of a stranger I will not listen."
With emphasis I said,
"I know the peace His presence brings,
I know when I have a desire for anything
According to Your will
You never hesitate to give.

I think often of you,

Your love pours in me by Your Spirit
So I can love others too,
Your compassion flows from You to me
So I can do, in any situation what you would do.

Like forgiving one another, when they miss it with me,
By doing something, that really did hurt deeply,
I know when I forgive them, you forgive them too.

I think of you often,

And it puts me in a place
That comforts and strengthens me for a new day
I like to think of you often,
Because you think even more of me

I think of you often,

It keeps me close to you,
And you know,
That's where I always want to be.

Intimate Moments

An Appointed Time with Him Alone

Go out and spend some time in a special place you and Our Heavenly Father alone. It's a date! An appointed time!
Look! Listen! Enjoy!

Do not make any excuses. Just do it!

_____
_____
_____
_____
_____
_____
_____
_____
_____
_____
_____
_____
_____

I Am Naked

In my created state
Pure and Holy I stood before you
As a creature
That knew no sin
Outward or within.

Blood washed.
Woman,
I am naked
Once again
By Jesus' blood
I am cleansed,
In His righteousness
I now stand.

I behold Him,
I behold who I am in Him.
Fully aware
Without Him, I am nothing

Help me O'Lord
Woman that I am
Reflect you to others
Keep me
Under your cover.

You are my first
You are my last
My whole existence.

In you my past is my past
In you is where my future begins.

My daily invitation
Reign in me
That I may remain
Naked
 pure and holy

Blood washed
Woman
Once again
By Jesus' blood
I am cleansed.

I am Naked
I am hidden in You.
You know all that I am from beginning to end.

I Love Nothing More Than God

I love nothing more than God
What he has for me is good
What he does for me is good
What he is to me is good

What is there not to love?
He Himself is good.
God is love.

He pleases my entire being
I thirst to drink from His fountain
He has plenty to give to me
He calls me early in the morning,
Subtle mid-day kisses of life's sweetness
Reminds me that he is with me.
In evening moonlight
My soul pants and He holds me as I
Slip into a peaceful rest in His arms.
And when the morning comes just before dawn
He invites me to dine at the breakfast
Nook
I sit,
My spiritual belly is filled
I am blessed to be a blessing on each path I take.

When I leave his presence
He opens doors that
His light may illuminate from me to expose the
The darkness wherever I go.

From my belly
Words of encouragement flow
My purpose is only Him
No matter where I am
Even when my paths seem stony
I am here by His authority
I do His will and He takes care of me
I am worriless.

My mind is engulfed with pleasure to serve you
I feel your gesture like a wink of a proud Father
You are pleased as I choose to obey your commands

Someone called me because they needed you in the flesh
So I obeyed you and yielded
You stirred the gifts and changed defeat to victory
One word spoken in season
Meeting the need

I love nothing more than God
What is there not to love?
He is love to us all.
And being there for a friend
Reassures them of His goodness
And His promise He will never forsake them
I know they see you when I stand
They see they can make it too
Right in the midst of storms and trials
I decided to smile because
My soul is satisfied
I have obeyed
I choose to keep my head up
In that I can't see defeat
For God so loves me
He gave His Son
All my enemies, He defeats
So I love nothing more than God.

Intimate Moments

_____
_____
_____
_____
_____
_____
_____
_____
_____
_____
_____
_____
_____
_____

Reflections

Can you see God's Woman?

The Naked Life

Genesis 2:25

"The man and his wife were both naked, and they felt no shame."

In this paradise they walked together naked and un-
ashamed. When you are naked you have nothing between
you and the person or objects next to you. They were in
perfect harmony with one another and with God. Here we
are in our original form. No disorder, no fear, no exclu-
sions from our creator, God.

We are going to take another look at how we were so we
can get back to who we are as "God's Woman". Eve was
the veteran of life's pleasures. She did not know embarrass-
ment, envy, jealousy, bitterness, and all the emotional is-
sues we encounter today. She had a "taste" of God himself.

I want you to know and understand two things. The first
thing is that tasting of the Lord and seeing that He is good
was not limited to Eve. The second thing is that tasting and
seeing that the Lord is good did not end with Eve. This is
what God is telling us now.

Psalm 34:7-9

*"The angel of the LORD encamps around those who fear him,
and he delivers them.
Taste and see that the LORD is good;
blessed is the man who takes refuge in him.
Fear the LORD, you his saints,
for those who fear him lack nothing."*

*W*hen we make a fervent step to establish our relationship by reconnecting to God we get to taste of God's goodness. God's goodness is an attribute of Himself. Goodness is a quality that belongs to God and a quality that we can always accredit to Him.

The fervency of my heart is being God's Woman every day in all things. One thing about this phenomenality desire in me is it never stops. Everyone that comes into the Body of Christ can experience the Presence of God, and can acquire an earnest desire to become more, moving beyond the minute issues and becoming God's individual whether male or female, young or old. He would not invite us in to be left empty, lacking or void. Look at all of what God is saying here.

Psalm 34:7-9
"The angel of the LORD encamps around those who fear him,
and he delivers them.
I protect you.
Taste and see that the LORD is good;
blessed is the man who takes refuge in him.
I bless you, I am here for you.
Fear the LORD, you his saints,
for those who fear him lack nothing."

I provide your every need. You can trust Me.

What a Father! What a God!

I meditated on this scripture I became persuaded of the goodness of God.

"O' taste and see that the LORD is good", the result of tasting of the LORD is finding out that He is good. First of all this scripture instructs and informs. It instructs us to "taste" and exactly what to taste of. It informs us that once we taste of the LORD we are des-

tined to "see" that He is nothing but "good". The word taste lets us know that you have entered in an awareness of something (in this case) something greater, you have conceived something greater, consequently; an unquenchable desire has now developed in you.

When babies are born the first type of food for them is milk. As children grow, their diets change. In the next stage the baby is usually given cereal, after that solid baby foods, following those stages the child finally gets to what we African Americans would call "soul food" which is table food, however; it had been our experience if a baby had a little taste of what was good (soul food or table food) he entered into an awareness there is something greater and he developed an unquenchable desire for it.

I will share my experience of what happened with our first child. As parents my husband and I always believed in keeping our children ourselves. If we had to go somewhere our children weren't exempt because they were our responsibility. Yes we planned our activities around what or where our children could be a part. There are times you will need someone else to aid you and there were times that people just want to keep our children. By the way, people enjoy well-behaved children. Well, my sister kept our daughter around the age of five or six months. That was the age grandma would always say "give that baby some food off the table, it's not going to hurt them". We had chosen not to change her diet yet.

After her stay with my sister we noticed she was no longer satisfied with what we were giving her. Later her sweet Aunt informed us that she had a "taste" of what was good, "soul food". We learned from that experience what kind of encounters our other two children could experience with their sweet aunt.

When we come into the Presence of God we will receive a taste for something greater. I have experienced the Goodness of God and my fervent desire is being God's Woman always in all things. Again, my prayer for every person in Christ now and those to come is to become His individual.

Let me explain what the Presence of God is. The presence of God is the Glory of God and the Glory of God is synonymous to the Goodness of God. Do you remember in the scriptures when Moses asked God to show him His Glory and God said I will show you my *"Goodness"* (Exodus 33:14, 18, 22)?

"My presence will go with you and I will give you rest" v.14

"I will make all My Goodness pass before you" v.18

Then He said,

"So shall it be while My Glory passes" v. 22

What did God say would pass before Moses? He said "His Goodness". What did He say it shall be that pass? He said "His Glory". So what is He saying? Go back to verse 14, He said "My Presence shall go with you", therefore; I submit to you that the Presence of God is the Glory of God and the Glory is synonymous to the Goodness of God.

We see here that *"tasting"* is a key to develop a fervent desire for God and his goodness.

How do you taste of the Lord? Simply asking Him into your life is the beginning of tasting of Him. Remember, in the beginning I said, "I had a phenomenal desire. I yearned to know God." When I was being drawn from the world into the kingdom of God a taste was developing in me. The next step is to get into the right fellowship, church. Find a church that will teach you the uncompromising Word of God and demonstrate it in love and action by example. Focus on God. Take time to pray, and ask for the Holy Spirit and wisdom. He will come and He will guide you in your walk just as He does for many others and me. Grow in your commitment to learn the Word of God for yourself. Your life depends on it. Success, the success of your spiritual destiny will depend on this. When the enemy comes and presents unpleasant encounters in and outside the church you will need to know God. Knowing Him and knowing His voice will help you. It will be times that you will have to decide for yourself to only listen to Him and to focus only on Him to make it.

What Adam and Eve experienced with God and with one another is what we have to look forward to. In the meantime, we have a life through Jesus (by our own commitment and faithful desire to choose His way in all things) which is good, peaceable, and abundantly blessed while we are on the earth. He wants us to have a naked life, perfect harmony with Him and one another lacking none of His Goodness.

God's woman is a woman that has reconnected, through Jesus, her relationship with Him. This is a first priority and desire. She keeps Him first.

Don't Listen To The Devil

It was not until Eve listened to her adversary, Satan, that she, and everyone that came after her, began to experience life as we see it today. She became separated from God as people are today.

Satan was formally called "Lucifer." Let's see why he plotted to put a stop to this union that God created among His creation. Why he chose to speak to the woman?

Let's look at Satan's formal status with God. He lived in the heavenly place with God and ministered to Him. He knew God.

Ezekiel 28:12-16

12 "Son of man, take up a lamentation for the king of Tyre, and say to him, 'Thus says the Lord GOD: "You were the seal of perfection, Full of wisdom and perfect in beauty. 13 You were in Eden, the garden of God; Every precious stone was your covering: The sardius, topaz, and diamond, Beryl, onyx, and jasper, Sapphire, turquoise, and emerald with gold. The workmanship of your timbrels and pipes was prepared for you on the day you were created. 14 You were the anointed cherub who covers; I established you; Can you see how God created him so wonderfully and how he must feel now? You were on the holy mountain of God; You walked back and forth in the midst of fiery stones. 15 You were perfect in your ways from the day you were created, Look where he was with God. Till iniquity was found in you. 16 " By the abundance of your trading You became filled with violence within, And you sinned; Therefore I cast you as a profane thing Out of the mountain of God; And I destroyed you, O covering cherub, From the midst of the fiery stones.

Look how sin can change a thing.

Let's look at life after the fall of man. Look at these scriptures again.

Ezekiel 28:15-16
*15 You were perfect in your ways from the day you were
created, Look where he was with God. Till iniquity was
found in you. 16 " By the abundance of your trading You
became filled with violence within, And you sinned; There-
fore I cast you as a profane thing Out of the mountain of
God; And I destroyed you, O covering cherub,
From the midst of the fiery stones.*

I think it's safe to say, that God was not longer pleased with Lucifer, (now Satan). I would say after God had created man and gave Him likeness to Himself and authority, Satan was disgusted and jealous. You know how it is said that we women are sometimes. Woman of God meets a good man, gets blessed with a home, nice car, or any of these blessings. The word is out. There is nothing good that Sister Jealous can find to say about her sister in the Lord. The plot is on. Sister Jealous is going to try all she can to destroy her character and her. This is sad but very true of some people in the Body of Christ. But God gives us a way of escape through love.

Genuine love is not jealous. We must learn to choose what is good in the sight of God. "If it is not good, it is not God." So, instead of criticism, rejoice with her and expect your blessing because God has no respect of persons.

The trait of Sister Jealous is that of Satan--steal, kill, and destroy. It is of the devil. As members of the body of Christ we are to edify one another. In other words it is better to say nothing than to criticize and plot against one another. We are supposed to add to each other. This is what makes us a strong body of believers. Let me give you something to help you here.

Admit to yourself that this is a problem in your life. Then admit your sin to God and ask for forgiveness and deliverance. God will help you change. Whenever you are tempted to say or do something wrong, stop right there and say; "This is not God. I am created in the image of God and I have the choice to do as He would in this situation." You will then see yourself getting blessed. This is not easy, but if you practice doing it, it will become a good habit.

We just have to remember that in all things there is a choice. I had some issues that I am not proud of and I know now that I can't change them, however; I can change the way I view them. And if others don't forget them I know for myself that those issues are under my feet. I use them to continue to step above where I was. I carry a better image of myself because when God forgave me I moved right back into righteousness with Him.

Today I refuse to allow Satan to have victories that were given to me. Jesus paid a high cost. Since I am destined to be God's Woman, I must walk worthy of that calling at all cost. You might think that God's Woman thinks highly of herself, no, God does. So I think as God thinks of me. No more defeats. I began to realize that my thinking of myself had to be extraordinary. I am highly favored and loved by God. What He has for me is mine.

This was the way that Satan saw man. Highly confident having a grand life and relationship with God. He knew what that was like.

Genesis 3:1-19
1 Now the serpent was most crafty than any of the wild animals the LORD God had made. He said to the woman, "Did God really say, 'You must not eat from any tree in the garden'?"

Don't listen to the devil.

2 The woman said to the serpent, "We may eat fruit from the trees in the garden, 3 but God did say, 'you must not

*eat fruit from the tree that is in the middle of the garden,
and you must not touch it, or you will die.' " 4 "You will
not surely die," the serpent said to the woman. 5 "For God
knows that when you eat of it your eyes will be opened, and
you will be like God, knowing good and evil."*

I see this as a passive moment that cost us all. Eve's guard was down when Adam (the male) did not step forward in his position of authority over Satan before Eve responded to him and took of the fruit. This reveals the importance of our head covering us today. This also reveals the importance of men, to be godly men standing in their position of authority and to teach it to their sons.

*6 When the woman saw that the fruit of the tree was good
for food and pleasing to the eyes, and also desirable for
gaining wisdom, she took some and ate it. She also gave
some to her husband, who was with her, and he ate it. 7
Then the eyes of both of them were opened, and they real-
ized they were naked; so they sewed fig leaves together and
made coverings for themselves. 8 Then the man and his
wife heard the sound of the LORD God as he was walking
in the garden in the cool of the day, and they hid from the
LORD God among the trees of the garden. 9 But the LORD
God called to the man, "Where are you?" 10 He answered,
"I heard you in the garden, and I was afraid because I was
naked; so I hid." 11 And he said, "Who told you that you
were naked? Have you eaten from the tree that I command-
ed you not to eat from?" 12 The man said, "The woman
you put here with me—she gave me some fruit from the tree,
and I ate it." 13 Then the LORD God said to the woman,
"What is this you have done?" The woman said, "The
serpent deceived me, and I ate." 14 So the LORD God said
to the serpent, "Because you have done this, "Cursed are
you above all the livestock and all the wild animals! You
will crawl on your belly and you will eat dust all the days
of your life. 15 And I will put enmity between you and the
woman, and between your offspring and hers; he will crush*

your head, and you will strike his heel." 16 To the woman
he said, "I will greatly increase your pains in childbear-
ing; with pain you will give birth to children. Your desire
will be for your husband, and he will rule over you." 17 To
Adam he said, "Because you listened to your wife and ate
from the tree about which I commanded you, 'You must not
eat of it,' "Cursed is the ground because of you; through
painful toil you will eat of it all the days of your life. 18 It
will produce thorns and thistles for you, and you will eat
the plants of the field. 19 By the sweat of your brow you
will eat your food until you return to the ground, since from
it you were taken; for dust you are and to dust you will
return." 20 Adam named his wife Eve, because she would
become the mother of all the living. 21 The LORD God
made garments of skin for Adam and his wife and clothed
them. 22 And the LORD God said, "The man has now be-
come like one of us, knowing good and evil. He must not be
allowed to reach out his hand and take also from the tree of
life and eat, and live forever." 23 So the LORD God ban-
ished him from the Garden of Eden to work the ground from
which he had been taken. 24 After he drove the man out, he
placed on the east side of the Garden of Eden cherubim and
a flaming sword flashing back and forth to guard the way
to the tree of life.

Listening to the devil only leads you away from God and all that He has for you. God's Woman is in every woman. She must connect with God. She's revealed through listening and obeying God in the face of trials and temptations. In other words, she's revealed right in the face of the devil when she takes a stand and loves God more.

We've talked about Eve being the first woman and the fact that she experienced life first hand with God Himself. Now let's look at another part of her role as the mother to all. Her name means, "life giving". She was purposed to bring us into a wonderful life giving experience with God. Sin ended that perfect state.

After the fall she began to experience life as we do. She began to experience a life that the nature of sins would endure. In her perfect state she had pleasures and joys all the time. But after sin she had sorrows. Let's take a look at those now.

Her first sorrow was the lost of relationship as it was perfect between her husband and God. There was nothing missing, nothing lacking. Her disobedience caused the broken relationship with God. That made things a mess. And we still experience the repercussions of man's sin today, although, we have the connection available for us to have a relationship through the blood of Jesus. Everything suffered when she sinned. She passed it on to Adam and all of God's children thereafter.

Her second experience of sorrow was a lost of a perfect home. She and Adam were banished from home. Imagine something better than your dream home and an unlimited account of provisions. Imagine having everything available all the time, and then to become homeless to life as it was. What a transition, but God in all of His goodness, still loves us through our disobedience.

The third sorrow was the lost of her children. Yes, I said children. We always recall that Abel was murdered by his brother but Cain, also became a run away. Imagine your child gone or just a child out there away from home. This is a painful experience for a parent. Children, whether teens, or young adults, and even older adults (all parents love to hear from them, like God, parents desire all things to be well with their children. Parents pray for them but they also like to hear their voice throughout the week. Never get too busy for that.

Just like Eve our lives can have sorrowful events. Remember that God is a good and loving God that never changes.

Malachi 3:6 NKJ
"For I am the Lord I do not change"

Although Adam and Eve sinned, Gods love for them never departed. As we read Genesis 3. We can look at the scriptures and see God giving them and Satan the consequences of their actions. Still, look at God's provision for His children.

Genesis 3:21 NKJ
"The LORD God made clothing from animal skins for Adam and his wife."

This truly reveals His love. This also lets us know today that He is a forgiving God. No matter what sorrows we experience God is a loving, forever present Father that desires to take us through to our victory.

As women we experience undesirable acts toward us. Those acts can be injected by friends, children, spouse, boss, co-workers, or anyone, but now's the time to realize that trying to get back is not the reaction God wants from us. God's women will not respond that way. Remember that choice is what we face.

Don't stop your healing.

Don't stop you financial blessings.

Don't stop the things you are expecting.

Stop Satan!

You may say, "I had a situation and I didn't respond as God would or as God's woman." So can many of us. What determines if we are God's woman is our choice from that point. Repent. Remember what I said previously. When God forgives you, you move right back into righteousness with Him. I keep saying this because we are challenged when we miss it. We are challenged in our minds on what we are now. Satan wants us to think less of who we are so we can lose sight of our identity in Christ and be defeated. Repent, and when we do this from the heart, God knows and He is the one that matters. He sees the heart. The heart is where truth can be found good or bad, truth is there.

Four things to remember when you face undesirable events:

1. Forgiveness: forgive yourself, forgive others, and do not think that you are less of an individual. Ask others to forgive you even when they are wrong.

2. Love: love at all times. Love will never fail you. Love is an action, so do it!

3. God is with you.

4. You win.

Satan is a liar. There is no truth or good that can be found in him. Jesus even told us that.

"The thief does not come except to steal, to kill, and to destroy. I have come that they may have life, and that they may have it more abundantly." John 10:10

When we allow love to prevail the true treasures of life will be seen in us.

"but lay up for yourselves treasures in heaven, where neither moth nor rust destroys and where thieves do not break in and steal."

Love is a valuable treasure; if you don't give it as God does you don't have it.

Our genuine love produces obedience. Genuine love gives no matter what and it pours like a river from the heart.

Don't listen to the devil! You are God's Woman in His love and obedience.

Intimate Moments

_____
_____
_____
_____
_____
_____
_____
_____
_____
_____
_____
_____
_____
_____
_____
_____
_____
_____
_____
_____
_____
_____
_____
_____

Poetic Meditations

Part 3

A Moment to Reflect on God's Goodness
And Who You Are

Eve's Past - Our Future

Imagine then,
Imagine now.
Imagine the sorrow she felt
    After knowing how things
    Could have been
    If she had not sinned.
Imagine her first tears and joys
    In childbirth's pain
    Now that childbirth changed.
Imagine watching
    Her children play with one another
    Then to see the bloodshed lost
    And the wondering heart of a mother
    Of a run away child.
Imagine looking back to better
    And facing the result of
    One bad choice.
Imagine her Father still loving her
    After all the wrong
    Then forgiven.
Imagine you and I having
Every opportunity to have what she had
Now to look forward to
The reward of life with God
But we too have the choice
She had
To obey.

Life Lessons

- Value who you are now.

- Do not focus on your pass.

- Renew your mind in the word of God regularly.

- Accept the original view and truth of who you are. God's view.

- Let the word of God define you.

- God will not restore your physical virginity but he will restore you, in Him you are righteous and holy and worthy of His best.

- Give God your best in all aspects of your life.

God's Woman's Journal/ Study Time
(Find the scripture in the Bible that supports these life lessons)

_____
_____
_____
_____
_____
_____
_____
_____
_____
_____
_____
_____

You Are A Masterpiece

You are a Masterpiece,
A work of art,
Unique in every way.
Kind and gentle,
A joy to another's day.
A sure work of the Master's hand.

You are a Masterpiece
A special design
Whether you are a man, woman, boy, or girl
You are, one of a kind.

I see the work of His hands upon you life,
As you seek and strive to grow in Him each day.
Your decisions reflect Him well.
A willingly yielded vessel
 In the palm of the Master's Hand.

You are a Masterpiece
A work of art,
To His completion,
One of a kind,
Made in His image,
Truly the work of the Master's Hand
Filled with His Spirit,
 Placed in the earth
To fulfill the Master's plan.
You are a Masterpiece.

You are a Masterpiece
A sure work of the master's Hand.
Pick up your cross and follow the Master's Plan.

My Garments Speak

What does my garment say?
      Who do my garments speak to?
Or is it really
      me talking?

Is this all I have?

My garments have expressions
      Did I take the time to listen to them?
      Or did I even care?

It's cute! It will fit well!
But does it?

Do they say what God says about me?
Does it tell of my virtue?
Or do they remove all the value that
 God places on me.
Do I even know or,
      Do I reject what I know?
Do I reject the voices of purity, honor, and self-respect, value and worth?

I am a bride to be...
  Will my groom recognize me?

  Do they underline date rape potential?
      Will my groom have anything left
          That I have not exposed in my choice of apparel
      To call his own?

My integrity,
The right attitude identifies something special about me,
They are my inward apparels.

Why should my outward garments speak so loud?
      They are seen from afar, and before I speak, they do!

Love covers me and teaches me.

So, I choose what~
      ~My Garments Speak.

Sanctified Santuary

Set apart
Sanctified
Purposed
For one man of your dreams

You are His beloved first
You are his beloved only

When your table is set
Only you shall dine
In that holy place
You and he alone
In His presence.

Visitors should never tour
Holy and undefiled
Sanctified sanctuary
Preserved for you to minister
To one another there

You shall celebrate
Enjoy the fruit of this sanctified place
And blossom there
This is your
Sanctified Sanctuary

Queens & Princesses

In so many ways we set the example to others. Our voices are heard when we think we are being silent. This lets us know our character should always exemplify our Heavenly Father. When we miss it, admit it; don't quit, just get back in place immediately.

We are teaching others all the time. Look around you, there are many dreamers. Our little girls want to be a princess, show them a queen. Our job as women is to tell them who they are through our lives. It's not a Cinderella idea we want to birth in them. Instead we want them to know, who God created in them. There are many God-led Biblical examples of wholesome qualities. Read about them then define your qualities. Ask yourself, "Are these qualities of value to the next generation of God's Woman, our little princesses now?"

My life embodies a particular character trait that Abigail had, strength. Her name means "My Father's Joy". Now that does not mean that I have the exact life that she had. It means that I have the character trait that she exhibits, in my life's experiences.

In this book it is my passion for woman to just genuinely love one another. This is the character trait "of the joy of Priscilla," meaning "worthy or venerable". She reveals destiny and design to me. She had joy in spreading the gospel and nurturing the church. She was valuable to Paul's life and in her world she made a difference.

"Greet Priscilla and Aquila, my fellow workers in Christ Jesus. They risked their lives for me. Not only I, but all the churches of the Gentiles are grateful to them." Romans 16:3

Now, I want to be introduced, Please Greet God's Woman Sharon. As Paul wrote, what are we writing on the heart of others about us?

Aim To Please

God's grace and mercy follows us all the days of our lives. His love endures in all circumstances. What a wonderful Father. I can't say that enough simply because I know He loves me so much. We need his love. My aim is to please Him.

In the natural realm, fathers have an important role. Depending on circumstances, they may or may not fulfill the role. Life outside of the kingdom of God removes life's best simply because we accept what is not in the will of God. At that time we are not really focusing on the consequences for others or ourselves. I did it and so did you, while living outside of a relationship with God. When we disobey we step right back into that realm, leaving our place of righteousness. As I write these things I want you to understand one profound thing that I've learned "Satan is at the root of all evil and every wrong." Yes, he presents things well. But we just have to make every effort to choose God.

There were things that altered my daily relationship with my natural father but it didn't alter his love for me. Isn't that an awesome revelation and example of the way God is towards us? I love my father immensely and I knew as a child and even more now, how deep down that he loves me too. I believe even in hard times that love breaks through and help you along the way. I can rejoice in God's goodness because His love can devour the pain of the flesh and recreate a unity of love.

We all have a story. In life we can encounter repercussions from choices that were not even our own, but God heals and brings you to a place of strength and love for Him. For me, my life, God gets the glory. He is the one that walks with me daily and keep His healing and loving hand upon me no matter what I face. The other side of that profound thing I've learned is, "God is at the beginning, the end, and everywhere in between and if we operate with His heart of love you will win every time."

Like I said we all have a story but I say this to say that our roles in life are many and whatever it is we must seek God to help us be authentic in them so that He may be seen.

As women we can relate. Our roles sometime seem to exceed our shoes and for some women, that's a lot. Whatever role God has predestined for you; woman, friend, wife, mother, career person, sister, and on and on; they all have their significant aim to please God. Everyone else will adjust; they may even call you blessed.

God said, *"love the Lord your God with all your heart, with all your soul, and with all your might"* (Luke 10:27). When He tells us this, He also tells us of the blessing that will follow.

I believe that understanding the role of "woman" is the foundation to our success in everything else. What am I saying? Being a woman of God involves our personal walk with the security of knowing who we are. Unless we, first, identify ourselves with Him we will not be all we are destined to be. We are divine, destined and purposed. We have our own destiny as a woman. Being God's woman is putting God first in all, being established in who he created you to be. That pleases Him.

Often time women will lock themselves in their roles and those roles become their identity instead of that which God created them to be-- individuals with divine purpose in the earth. Do not misunderstand this, we are to be great wives, mothers, career persons, and etc. but be it with God first. Our connection with God connects us with our divine purpose in life. Without a connection to God we cannot please Him nor fulfill anything to its full potential.

God invested Himself into us. We must please Him while being pleased with ourselves. How do we do that? We start by seeing ourselves through His eyes.

Think back to the beginning, when God looked at all of creation and called it "good." We are a part of His creation. Treasure how He took the time to perfect us. Recall how He created us to be rightly desired. Then look at what He said, woman would be, a help meet. We have a gift of meeting needs through our roles. As a wife, we aid and assist our mates. It's our own mates that we aim to please not someone else's mate. God really is serious about how we handle one another. Have you read Ephesians 5: 22-31 lately?

22 Wives, submit to your own husbands, as to the Lord. 23 For the husband is head of the wife, as also Christ is head of the church; and He is the Savior of the body. 24 Therefore, just as the church is subject to Christ, so let the wives be to their own husbands in everything.

25 Husbands, love your wives, just as Christ also loved the church and gave Himself for her, 26 that He might sanctify and cleanse her with the washing of water by the word, 27 that He might present her to Himself a glorious church, not having spot or wrinkle or any such thing, but that she should be holy and without blemish. 28 So husbands ought to love their own wives as their own bodies; he who loves his wife loves himself. 29 For no one ever hated his own flesh, but nourishes and cherishes it, just as the Lord does the church. 30 For we are members of His body, of His flesh and of His bones. 31 "For this reason a man shall leave his father and mother and be joined to his wife and the two shall become one flesh."

I will suggest a reading like this one more often. You know sometimes we just miss things with God by not renewing our minds in the areas of life that are our own.

Basic Essentials Of God's Woman

Some may think that a woman's basic essentials are her make-up, apparel, nails, and spa treatments and of course her shoes and bags. Yes, they are important and personally I have a few others on my list of essentials but please let me share some essential points in our role as women, especially as God's Woman.

There are four basic essentials that I will share with you.

1. Build a strong foundational relationship with God.
2. Develop a strong confidence in the Word of God.
3. Keep your focus on God here and in every role that become a part of your life.
4. Never lose confidence in God and His word no matter what.

I know that these essential points might sound redundant, but look at the content of each statement.

Basic Essential #1 Build a strong foundational relationship with God.

We saw in creation how important our relationship with God first is so, building a strong foundation with God, as a woman, takes more than going to church listening to the man or woman of God. It takes individual dedication to the Word and time with God. If you were going to build a house in the natural the foundation would be constructed after prior preparation for it. But once the building starts the foundation is properly prepared so that all the other parts thereafter will be able to withstand the house and all its other contents. Spiritually this is where the rubber meets the road in life. We must have a strong foundation to stand in the roles that we are destined to walk in. There will be challenges and our strength will come from what is rooted on the inside of us.

"My people are destroyed by the lack of knowledge."
Hosea 4: 6

Basic Essential #2, 3, and 4

Develop a strong confidence in the Word of God. Focus. Don't lose Confidence in God.

Developing a strong confidence in the Word of God will come from spending time in the Word. But the truth is revealed when the storms come. Will you have the confidence in the Word to use it to conquer the storms? Will you have peace? Or will your confidence and peace be blown away with the wind before the storm's mightiest force come in?

For example one storm I experienced was following an annual physical and an annual mammogram. Around eight years ago I had an adverse report from my mammogram. This report revealed a sighting that required another examination. This was the wind that came before the storm for me. How I reacted from the moment that I picked up the phone to the moment that I returned to be retested was a fierce battle of the mind. It was that moment that I knew what it meant *"the violent take it by force"*. I had to be violent about my faith concerning wholeness of body. The devil suggested I worry. He (remember don't listen to the devil) tried to tell me I had cancer, beyond that I would die.

My faith overpowered the suggestions, however; multiple daily suggestions never stopped. My prior experience with God's faithfulness, knowing that God is a God that cannot lie or does he change or have a respect of persons and knowing Him was the foundation I had to stand on. Why? It was all truth that the Word of God supported. I used healing scriptures and tapes to reinforce the trust I had in God. I had a benign tumor. I had to have surgery and Satan kept on lying, lying, lying "you are going to die." He used this because of past experiences that gave me fear. The surgery was successful of course. By now you ought to know, I am a girl with a plan, a person with a mission, and God's Woman with a destiny to complete. To God be all the glory. Listen, if God had not been my strong tower for so many other things as well as having being taught so well concerning faith and trusting God. I would have fainted at the moment I received the call.

It is times like these that we know that we have nothing else but God. I know that there is nothing better than God; honestly through the natural eye this is not the position we want to be in. The key is to have that confidence before the storms come. When my son was very sick and for no apparent reason, when my daughters fell ten feet through the ceiling, and when my daughter became sick and again no understanding what was happening nor why?

When my son walked out the door and said see you later mom and less than five minutes I received a phone call saying he's been in an accident where the car was crushed and flipped. It appeared as no one could possibly have survived, but he came out with, only, a scratch on the hand. When facing another disease and tumors and experiencing known hatred, my sails have been torn nearly to pieces. Love prevails. Just knowing my wonderful Father is carrying me helps me to press on. These are my testimonies and with the Word of God; my life has reinforcements that help me keep faith in God.

If I would give my life a name it would probably be Abigal meaning "My Father's Joy" and because her character demonstrated great peacemaker, her ministry. God used her to save lives. I see clearly ahead what God has been saying to me "I will honor you as you have consistently been generous, willing, and continue on the right path no matter how difficult, I honor those who are faithful even when faithfulness brings difficulty, hardship, and pain."

Psalm 30:10-12

Hear, O LORD, and be merciful to me;
O LORD, be my help."
11 You turned my wailing into dancing;
you removed my sackcloth and clothed me with joy,
12 that my heart may sing to you and not be silent.
O LORD my God, I will give you thanks forever.

Psalm 40:11

Do not withhold your mercy from me, O LORD;
may your love and your truth always protect me.

Isaiah 41: 10

So do not fear, for I am with you;
do not be dismayed, for I am your God.
I will strengthen you and help you;
I will uphold you with my righteous right hand.

Unlike Abigail, I have to say my husband is more like David, a man after God's heart.

We must remember that Jesus forewarns us that we will face test but we must remember that He took upon himself all for us to have victory in any situation every time. Allow the storms to strengthen you, not to break you down.

You know the phrase "she's a strong black woman," that somehow became a part of my character through association of what many people thought of me. It was expectancy; whereas, I found myself obligated to be strong.

There are so many times God has strengthen me in different situations to encourage others to the point of persuasion of their faith in God to come to Him, increase, and be established in Him; today I count it a blessing to see them grow continually in their faith. The lesson is to trust God beyond your own circumstances and not to focus on them but the answer to them, Him. When we do that, we can be valuable assets to God's Kingdom.

I hope that you can now see how building a strong foundational relationship with God is so vital to our success in all things. You should also see how building a strong confidence in the Word of God will only come with your commitment and determination not only to grow spiritually but to win all the time; therefore, focus and confidence is essential.

Ask yourself questions. Did I pray today? Did I have a personal fellowship with God, praise, worship, and read or listen to the word today? If not, I missed something. I missed fellowship and when I do I lose my part for increasing relationship. Our desire to be with Him will only increase in knowing Him.

As God's woman we must have a relationship with Him.

Immoral Or Virtuous

A Choice

Woman or man you can choose to be dishonest, wicked, or cor-
rupted. You can choose to be good, honorable, or upright. Which
one you choose is up to you. Biblically speaking, you can choose
to be immoral or virtuous. In the scriptures below we will see that
there is a description of two types of women. My point is not the
faith wife or the adulterous wife specifically but the character of the
two women in any situation.

Proverbs 2: 16-19

To deliver you from the immoral woman,
From the seductress who flatters with her words,
17 Who forsakes the companion of her youth,
And forgets the covenant of her God.
18 For her house leads down to death,
And her paths to the dead;
19 None who go to her return,
Nor do they regain the paths of life—

Proverbs 31:10-31

Who can find a virtuous wife?
For her worth is far above rubies.
11 The heart of her husband safely trusts her;
So he will have no lack of gain.
12 She does him good and not evil
All the days of her life.

These women are examples of good and bad character and influ-
ences. The immoral woman of course represents the ungodly and
the virtuous woman represents the godly woman. We are whom we
choose to be in life. Being God's woman is every woman's choice.
We can set our standard like the immoral or the virtuous woman.

God gives us choices all the time all the way back to the beginning. He will perfect who we are when we choose to obey His word.

The immoral woman forgets the covenant of her God. She does her own thing and what God desires for her is not on her agenda. She has bad influences. Her life leads to death. As I grow in the things of God I am becoming more virtuous inside and out. This is what I want for my life and for the lives of others.

Women can be by choice immoral, wicked. When our hearts are not sincerely turned towards pleasing God and when we have jealousies, when we are insecure, and when we are on the path of our own selfish agendas we are traveling down paths that are not pleasing to God. Now in the ungodly sense we know that these are the traits of Satan and we expect ugliness to come from a vessel that is his.

The virtuous woman is valuable in the sight of God and man. We can see from these examples who qualifies as God's woman. It is the woman that seeks the full potential of whom He created.

But the sad truth is that there are those that are proclaiming to be godly yet their acts are a portrait of an immoral woman. I pray that we all examine our hearts daily. If we are proclaiming godliness and find these things in us repent and turn from those wicked ways.

My life's lesson is:

Though Satan desires us and uses cunning devices to persuade us that compromising worldly attributes don't affect us, know that they do and those around us. If you are not saved your nature is that of the devil and you may not display these actions per se but living apart from God is death.

If you are a godly woman and have any of these hidden agendas in your heart, remember they are ungodly. God can see them. I urge you to repent now.

I am prompted by the Holy Spirit to say, if your circumstances have been very horrible which lead you down the paths of the ungodly and in turn has led you into a lifestyle that is not pleasing in the sight of God; you can be saved. God is able to clean everything in your life. Go ahead and put on the real you--God's woman. When you allow the peace of God to reign in your heart and forget the past you can be God's Woman, the woman that he purposed you to be. Go for it! You were meant to be a blessing.

Now lets look at God's Woman being blessed through obedience

Deuteronomy 28:1-3, 15-16

1 "Now it shall come to pass, if you diligently obey the voice of the LORD your God, to observe carefully all His commandments which I command you today, that the LORD your God will set you high above all nations of the earth. 2 And all these blessings shall come upon you and overtake you, because you obey the voice of the LORD your God: 3 "Blessed shall you be
15 "But it shall come to pass, if you do not obey the voice of the LORD your God, to observe carefully all His commandments and His statutes which I command you today, that all these curses will come upon you and overtake you:
16 "Cursed shall you be

The woman that seeks the full potential of whom He created can be the one that will become blessed and be a blessing.

The immoral woman is not faithful to her covenant with God. Her words are not trustworthy. Companionship with her is destructive. This is not the type of woman that I want to be nor does God want any of us to be. This is where we must take a stand in the body, as women of God and lead by the example of the Word of God fulfilling this scripture; *"the older women likewise, that they be reverent in behavior, not slanderers, not given to much wine, teachers of good things— 4 that they admonish the young women to love their husbands, to love their children, 5 to be discreet, chaste, homemakers, good, obedient to their own husbands, that the word of God may not be blasphemed."* Titus 2:3-5

God wants us all edifying in our walk toward one another. Our obedience becomes a blessing to the generations that follow us. When we uphold the call of God's Woman as a banner before young girls in our relationships among one another and in the ministry operating in integrity, harmony and love they will press toward the same goals. Ask yourself what example am I setting before the young ladies that are coming up? In your homes, are you bashing your sisters and plotting to sabotage their character? Repent! Again this is a choice. Our purpose is far greater and we as God's Woman have an obligation to demonstrate her everywhere at all the times so that others can see her and desire her.

I believe if, we as women can see ourselves as potential friends and not as rivals we will better serve the kingdom of God. What do we do to get to that point? You know it always begin with Him of course, why not? Romans 12:1-2 tells us how to present ourselves and not to be conformed to ways of the world and Titus 3:3 confirms that we are to maintain good works. We see in the following scriptures when His love and Spirit is activated in us we are able to let go of foolishness.

> *3 For we ourselves were also once foolish, disobedient, deceived, serving various lusts and pleasures, living in malice and envy, hateful and hating one another. 4 But when the kindness and the love of God our Savior toward man appeared, 5 not by works of righteousness which we have done, but according to His mercy He saved us, through the washing of regeneration and renewing of the Holy Spirit;* Titus 3:3-5.

This re-emphasizes many things that God is putting in my heart in relationship to being an instrument of unity and love among sisters; starting with prayer. Let's pray for each other. Create a sisterhood of prayer that will strengthen and increase the chain of godly women around the world. Why not become what we were created to be? Desired! Remember in the beginning. We know the power of prayer among women; let's activate the power of love among women in true unity instead of envy and hatefulness. Our acts of obedience will bring forth blessings in our lives and the lives of others.

Pray over your future friendships and your children's friendships as young ladies and godly women, we will find more joy among us.

Our positional relationship places a demand on us; love will cause us to carry it out. In other words, we may not become buddies, but our position in the body makes us sisters, we are both children of God. Though you and I may or may not know one another, you and I are connected by our heavenly Father thus, I rejoice with you and I esteem you in prayer and my thoughts of you are from God. I think of the exhortations that Paul said in regards to our positional relationship with one another in the following passages:

Philippians 4

Finally, brothers, [Christians] *whatever is true, whatever is noble, whatever is right, whatever is pure, whatever is lovely, whatever is admirable—if anything is excellent or praiseworthy—think about such things. Whatever you have learned or received or heard from me, or seen in me—put it into practice. And the God of peace will be with you.*

Rejoice in the Lord always. I will say it again: Rejoice! Let your gentleness be evident to all. The Lord is near. Do not be anxious about anything, but in everything, by prayer and petition, with thanksgiving, present your requests to God. And the peace of God, which transcends all understanding, will guard your hearts and your minds in Christ Jesus.

Keep these thoughts in mind.

Set the example of God's woman. You are blessed and you are a blessing through obedience and love. Please don't feel that this is a superficial action.

Authentic Sisters

Now that we have determined that our relationship to one another is positional to whom we are in Christ it's time to pick up the cross and follow Him authentically. God's Woman is authentic. Authentic is genuine or real. She will act like God and create a sisterhood rather than alienate her sisters in the Lord and people in general. I know that I am going over this again, but we must get this.

I know that there are women that have been victimized among the sisters and they act like there is nothing going on. I am ready to see the body of Christ doing it right. I have been out eating in restaurants, shoe shopping, sitting in the doctors' office even in public rest rooms, let me tell you, girls hate on one another. Now when it comes to the body it really hits a nerve.

I heard these conversations, my question is "Why you talk'n 'bout this and why are you so loud especially in public? Two things: they obviously don't realize they don't look good and they miss their blessing to having true fellowship with you and (ok a third thing, very important thing) if they don't get their love right they are going to miss out on God here on earth and in going to heaven; just because you are not operating in love, but hating on a sister.

Jesus gave us a command to follow, do as he does. Just imagine how it would be to have an authentic state of peace, love, and harmony in the body of Christ and specifically among the sisters? It is a responsibility of every woman of God. If we love God we will love each other.

If you have been victimized in some way, please understand you are only responsible for fully doing your part in spite of. We all are not going to be your best buddy but, we should have fellowship and be there for one another simply because God did not make us funny like that anyway.

What is the key to get our flow as authentic sisters together? Love.

Read 1 Corinthians 13 as we read it more and more it will get in our spirit and become more a part of us in action.
Remember, if we see ourselves as potential friends and not as rivals, we will serve the kingdom of God better.

Now I want to give you two keys to help you be an authentic sister in the body of Christ daily.

1. Build yourself up:
    • Get the plan of God for your life and be satisfied with what it is and build yourself up confidently in your own destiny.
    • Know that no one else can do what God destined for you.
    • Keep a servant's heart as God elevates you.
    • Stay sensitive to God.
2. Build up your resistance:
    • Insist on walking in genuine love at all times.
    • Don't walk in a spirit of competition towards others.
    • Stop the talk. Don't gossip.
    • See the people that are placed in your life as God's gift and potential friends or wonderful associates.
    • Go for it! Give genuine support to others in their gifts and talents. Even aid them in cultivating their gift, spiritually in prayer, physically help when there's a need or request, monetarily giving financial support. Mentally never become jealous of what God is doing in their lives.
    • Don't expect anything from them but their love, you may find yourself getting more.
    • Remember when things are happening for others it's their season and you have one coming too.
    • Do not get impatient with God.
    • Accept correction. Do not fall out of love with one another.
    • Remember that you are God's gift to them, make sure it remains in the condition that God packed it.
    • Build a spiritual hedge around yourself and your sisters.

Pray the above things over yourself and them.

Make a deposit in the lives of our sisters and embrace the rewards that God gives back to us through others in doing so.

When we learn to apply these things we become God's woman in the image of Him. Our lights become a glow upon us that draws others to God. We don't have to be like the way the world says women are "they don't get along."

But let me say this, you will have closer friendships than others but don't create clicks. Your associates could be the blessing you need to get to the next level of your walk. Let me tell you how to avoid the click chick thing. With your close friends enjoy them for who they are and don't ever allow yourself to talk about others. We uphold one another in love and truth.

Am I perfect? No, let's just press upward together. It's like this:

Philippians 3: 12-21 (MSG)
12-14 *I'm not saying that I have this all together, that I have it made. But I am well on my way, reaching out for Christ, who has so wondrously reached out for me. Friends, don't get me wrong: By no means do I count myself an expert in all of this, but I've got my eye on the goal, where God is beckoning us onward—to Jesus. I'm off and running and I'm not turning back.*
15-16 *So let's keep focused on that goal, those of us who want everything God has for us. If any of you have something else in mind, something less than total commitment, God will clear your blurred vision—you'll see it yet! Now that we're on the right track, let's stay on it.*
17-19 *Stick with me, friends. Keep track of those you see running this same course, headed for this same goal. There are many out there taking other paths, choosing other goals, and trying to get you to go along with them. I've warned you of them many times; sadly, I'm having to do it again. All they want is easy street. They hate Christ's Cross. But easy street is a dead-end street. Those who live there make their bellies their gods; belches are their praise; all they can think of is their appetites.*

20-21 But there's far more to life for us. We're citizens of high heaven! We're awaiting the arrival of the Savior, the Master, Jesus Christ, who will transform our earthy bodies into glorious bodies like his own. He'll make us beautiful and whole with the same powerful skill by which he is putting everything as it should be, under and around him.

You can start now. Pray with me. Lord, forgive me. I have not behaved as you would have me to in the past, but it stops right now. Help me to be authentic toward women and love them as you do. I refuse to operate in a spirit of division and disobedience. Thank you in Jesus name.

Press on in sisterhood (Holy Spirit inspired definition of sisterhood: a community of the same gender in relationship with God doing as her would toward one another.) uplifting each other in prayer to be God's Woman as women, wife, sister, mother and all the roles that our very own lives are destined to be.

Life lessons from the women in the Bible

- Mary became the mother to the Savior.

- Woman at the well believed on Him being the Messiah.

- Peter's Mother in-law received healing

- Widow of Nain, death could not hold her son when Jesus showed up with life. Luke 7

- Syrophenician Woman Matthew 15:21-28 and Mark 7:24-30

- Woman caught in Adultery Jesus saves and she sins no more. John 8:1-11

- Jesus sets Martha's priorities right Luke 10:38

- Widow with two coins models a lesson on giving Mark 12:41-44 / Luke 21:1-4

- Mary Magdalene faithfully follows Jesus Matthew 27:56,61 / 28:1 / Mark 15:40-47 / 16:1-11 / Luke 8:1-2 / 24:10 / John 19:25 / 20:1-8.

Get Your Bible Now! This is Important.

- Read Titus 2: 3-4 Whether young or old, women have the potential to affect her world and church by her character and the conduct of her life, these verses highlights the value of woman's influence and work.

1. Remember while reading these verses that this is not a restriction on a woman's role it is a picture of opportunity.

2. Being the creative godly woman that you are, remember you are to build a life where God's love can be experienced and seen through you causing others to thrive.

3. Remember: your faith is reflected.

4. Remember: moving beyond the home your character and your wisdom have broader influences on the world.

5. Remember: All this is achieved through godly character primarily, not domestic accomplishments. Though God's Woman has a valuable domestic role to her destiny.

   - Those that you know that are truly writing the words of the scripture with their life actions toward one another.

Poetic Meditations

Part 4

Reflect on God's Goodness
And Who You Are…
…God's Woman

God's Woman

I like to think
That every woman desires to be the best
in all the roles she plays
the best wife,
the best mother,
the best friend
the best woman, that's being the best me.
My desire is to be God's Woman
The one He created me to be.
I could view my life
In the natural but,
I wouldn't be able to see myself
Fulfilling such excellence of God's virtue in me.

The voices of this present world have enticed and seduced me,
Sometimes led me astray.
They desired me to recall each failure one by one,
With their hideous laughter they say,
"God's Woman' how could that ever be?"
But through Him I have unlimited possibilities.
With the ears of my spirit
I hear Him encouraging me.
Great joy raptures me.

A voice of thunder,
The Great and Mighty One
Captures my attention
"I've called you by name and led you out.
You belong to Me".
Forgiveness followed your confession
God's woman you shall be.
I've stripped away your sin and sanctified you,
Your life is now in Me.
Today your desire is fervent

I'm anointing you to have the words you say.
The world will recognize God's woman
In each role you play.
Your words will be of the wisdom
You bear in early meditations each day.
And upon your tongue the law of kindness
Toward those you encounter along the way.
You have watched over your household well,
Your work unique indeed,
But now my anointing will spur you to majestically succeed.
The beauty of God's woman isn't outward apparel.
It comes from within.
Sin no longer rules your heart
All that I have cleansed,
Although your outward apparel is of royalty
Your clothing is strength and honor.
One last thing right now I must say,
"Do not look back on yesterday's failure.
You are forgiven and my blood has washed them away.
Acknowledge and honor the Father in all you do and say.
Each path you take,
every role you play
with the Holy Spirit leading the way,
every person you encounter shall experience My presence because
God's woman
Has been and example of Me in all roles she play.

Prized

You are a precious jewel.
You are a queen.
You are prized.

> Do not be blinded by your residence.
> Do not be neglectful because of some financial absence,
> It's only a temporary matter.
> Do not be inattentive because of your apparel.

You are prized.

"Beauty is only skin deep" as the saying goes.
Real beauty originate inside out,
Although society generally
Doesn't vision it that way.

You are prized.

You are a precious jewel.
You are a queen.
You are prized.
You are your creator's special design.
 Crowned by Him.
Adorned in His Image.

> Come! Step out of the shadows of doubt.
> Inferiority has no reign.
> Come! Step out and see who you really are,
Highly esteemed.
Valued by God.
A Queen.
Come! Show the world with confidence that
You are prized.

Loving My Sister

Loving my sister is no different than loving
A spouse, a child, or God
Simply because
When God's love lives in me
It spills over to love others
No matter whom they are.

Love is a command
I'm to obey
If I am going to be God's Woman authentically
Loving my sister
Is the way
Lord I know
So I genuinely submit and obey
Loving my sister
 Your light through me will shine
  Reflecting
Your love so gentle and kind.

I'm Not Perfect

I'm Not Perfect
In the way that the world measures perfection
Unblemished
Faultless and complete
The perfect child
The perfect daughter
The perfect mother
The perfect wife
Or the perfect woman
Lacking nothing to the whole being
Of what I am
Human

I'm not perfect
Flawless in thought
Flawless in speech
Flawless in actions
Not even perfect in my appearance
As you think it should be

Though I've walked through life
Allowing a definition according
To standards that were not crucified
On the cross infiltrate my mind
And manipulate my actions

Trying to wash away the blemishes
According to the standards
You call perfect
Just to see the stains that appeared gone
Keep coming back
In that I am not perfect

Look at me
If all you see is the outward
Appearance of
Who you see
Me
Then you must lack perfection too.

Years ago a man of perfect status
Came down from glory
     Now get this
     It is far beyond a story
John 3:16 say, you know,
"For God so greatly loved and
dearly prized the world
that He [even] gave up
His only begotten (unique) Son,
 so that whoever believes in
(trusts in, clings to, relies on) Him
 shall not perish
 (come to destruction, be lost)
 but have eternal
 (everlasting) life"

Just like the woman
At the well, He told her to go
And sin no more,
Forgiveness came
And so did Jesus in my life.

He knocked at the door of misery
Found me trying to wash away
 the stains of life
that kept me bound
trying to scrub away the stains
of insecurity and   rejection cov-
ered
with false love
accepting the way that
another defined me.

But a voice from the depths
 Of my heart
And the throne room of God's
grace
 Reached out to set
Me free

I am not defined by
Un-crucified or unqualified means

Born of a virgin
Lived as the Son of Man
Crucified
He died
(for me)
Descended to the
The lower part of the earth
Rose on the third day
He led my captivity free
He sits at the right hand of the Fa-
ther
Making intercessions for me

And in that great and mighty day
He shall return
For the righteous
Those that are perfect under
His redeeming blood.

I have confessed my sins
Believed on Him
Picked up my cross
I follow Him.

I am not perfect
But l am
In Him.

Divine Attention! Domestic Formation

We know that the word domestic refers to the home, family, and household cares. Seldom do we think of domestic and divine together. Divine is godlike and extremely good. But, domestic duties like cooking; laundry, cleaning, etc..., are not ordinarily associated with godly pleasures as other luxuries of the blessings of God.

A few years ago I started praying and asking God to help me in the area of cooking. That was a tolerated chore for me. I began meditating on my ungodly attitude at heart. Recognizing this, I found this to be an undesirable trait. I had to address my heart attitude because it was part of my life. In perfecting God's woman you just have to keep it real. I cooked. I didn't really fuss. I just didn't like it. My husband cooks. My children do too. They seem to enjoy it and do it well. I specialize in specific dishes and holiday cooking.

Cooking wasn't a thing that I just like to do day to day. I wanted to feel differently because this was something that I felt, personally, was not satisfying in my life because of my attitude. Why didn't I take pleasure in it? I know we are not going to like everything but attitude is the focus. Cooking, being a part of my duties in my role as a wife and mother I thought, I might need to have a right heart toward it. I have been pleasantly spoiled in the area but it still does not change the importance of attitudes of the heart. What comes to mind is doing all things as unto the Lord. I love it when Joyce Myers says, "God wants you to enjoy your life," I take that to heart today. I'm not saying this to be a conviction for you in the area of domestic duties, but I am saying look at the way that we do things, heart matters. Then look at the other side to this coin, domestically are you being a good ruler over what God has given you.

1Chronicles 29:17
"I know also, my God, that You test the heart and have pleasure in uprightness. As for me, in the uprightness of my heart I have willingly offered all these things; and now with joy I have seen Your people, who are present here to offer willingly to You."

When I read these scriptures and others I think of what pleasure God has in a divine (God like) heart attitude.

"So let each one give as he purposes in his heart, not grudgingly or of necessity; for God loves a cheerful giver" (2 Corinthians 9:7).

"And whatever you do, do it heartily as to the Lord and not to men. Knowing that from the Lord you will receive the reward of the inheritance; for you serve the Lord Christ" (Colossians 4: 23-24).

As Christians the heart really matters in the things we do. I pursue my life to be all of what matters to God, because I know God's Woman desires to please Him in everything. I'm not perfect, but obedience perfects who we are. Our domestic responsibilities should also be of the heart.

How are you concerning domestic responsibilities and taking care of what God has given you where you are right now? We have the inclination of saying when I get the bigger house or more money what we will do better by it. Well doing better starts where we are right now, in whatever area of life we are dealing with.

Domestically when you imagine heaven do you see it cluttered, junky or just plain messy. I don't. I haven't ever heard nor read in the Bible where it gave any indication that it is disorganized. From the scriptures, its atmosphere is one to be desired. Our spiritual and physical homes should be in order.

I just ask our Father, "Is He pleased with the way I attend and carry out my duties domestically and I listen to be obedient to what He wants to improve in me more and more. It's my desire to bring pleasure to God in that area too.

I have work to do. We all have work to do. We must give our best in all things. We can't escape problems. We must solve them. This is obviously something God wants us to address, because I have to include it as a part of God's Woman. I think of it this way, if God wants to bless me and by way of an angel by night I don't want to miss it because of the clutter. For some woman, this is a real issue. God will help you get this part of you together if you ask Him.

So, stop avoiding your house, by leaving it, stop using TV, children and other projects as your distractions and no more appraisals-it's not that bad, yes it is, be honest you care and stop shopping to make it look better when you are just cluttering it up more. Do I need to go on Lord?

My specific problem was to overcome it. I recognized and admitted my problem. I prayed. I thought about my likes and dislikes. I like exotic things. I like certain plants that give me the atmosphere I love and the serenity I enjoy. Certain styles are just--me. So I figure; I can take that to my kitchen too. Just maybe the kitchen could be a place I would want to be. Voila! That was it. I incorporated different foods into my menus. And because I have not yet traveled to all the places I will one day, I began to watch travel and food programs periodically. I found myself enjoying the simple and exotic things I could do.

Look at me; I'm becoming more of God's woman in my kitchen. I chose to conquer that heart matter of a wrong attitude with pleasure. I realize that it may not take all of that for you, but for some of us it may. The important thing is really pleasing God from the heart.

This was my revelation and solution, so I built on it. For my matter of the heart I took practical action. First I created an atmosphere I enjoyed being in. I paid attention to the places I enjoyed eating and created a beautiful ambience. If you are married, consider your spouse--especially if he enjoys cooking.

1. Watch inspiring not compromising shows.
2. See yourself enjoying it.
3. Plan Ahead. (In the kitchen plan your meals)
4. Be creative and make your own dishes.
5. Be courageous and try new and exotic foods.
6. I love beautiful and different china (dishes) and the right cookware. So I bought some that I like looking at when I have to wash dishes.
7. Sometimes when I don't want to cook I order out and present it as nice as a home cooked meal.

Here are a few other domestic tips that will help us and remind us to be consistent in them.

- Make your bed as soon as it is empty.
- Put items back in their places as soon as you finish using them.
- Clear the table. Do the dishes immediately after eating
- This one is mine too. Handle the mail as soon as it arrives.
- Hang your clothes and put your shoes away when you take them off.
- Pray and ask God to make you visually sensitive to things that are out of place and fix them. Don't become a nag.
- Clean your desk (home office rescue) at the end of the day instead of leaving things out with the mind set I will be using this tomorrow. Cater this to your specific needs. The objective is to get rid of the clutter.

Father, help each of us use this as a way to make us better--not to become like one another. Give us the wisdom we need and package this knowledge to fit us as individuals. In Jesus' Name, Amen.

Remember: It's a heart matter I'm talking about. Our Father looks on the heart we should remember to "Do all things as unto the Lord and not unto man." When we do we can please both man and God.

Many women enjoy a nice home, but if our heart attitudes are not right, we won't enjoy what we have. I want to enjoy all of my life with the right attitude. I enjoy giving my guests an atmosphere to enjoy when they take time to visit my home. My husband and I work well together in doing this.

We can teach our boys and our girls how to give divine attention to our domestic duties.

God's woman is a teacher in life. Now, I want us to tap into this domestic resource to keep family unity and communication. Cooking, sewing and other crafts are slowly becoming lost arts no longer taught in our homes. I use cooking as an example because this is what I struggled with. Cooking is not part of our homes as parents due to the fast food generation. There is health value in cooking for our families. We will help their lives as they age if potential health values are taught early by us. The domestic area can reveal many things to us, such as our gifts. This is a way to recognize or discover them in ourselves and children. If we don't attend to these things with our children we can cause them to stumble, be lazy and delay finding their treasures while they are young.

Do you know that food is a way that we can minister love and care to our families as well? Think about mealtimes you had or you experienced with grandparents. Sitting down together can carry life long values. This is a time that the family communes. This is a way to stay in touch with one another. What if you can't cook? Practice. Practice. Practice. You don't have to be perfect, just give yourself the opportunity to be your personal best. You will eventually perfect something. Look back at the woman in Proverbs 31 and remember when I said I like exotic things. That is Biblical; "…she brings food from afar." This can provide you with variety.

Here's another tip that can be creative, fun and educational.

My family has done this. We decided on a different culture, searched for recipes and planned a menu around that specific culture. We invite guests and each family is then responsible for a historical fact about the culture. We even include games and attire. The children enjoy this and learn. The most important thing is the family gathering as well as trying new things. Each household leaves with a copy of the recipes to try at home. That really is creative, fun and educational! I can't wait for the next one!

Jesus broke bread with His disciples, so I am encouraged by His example.

1. Learn to take meal times to a new level with your family.
2. Make time for sharing and exchanging beyond Christmas.
3. Enjoy and lift up one another.
4. Keep the family together.

God's Woman is who we are. Our Father is a God of order. You know there is always something that we can improve on. As women in pursuit of being our best, we have to keep an open mind, so I make every effort to exercise wisdom in every area. Remember I'm not perfect, but recognition and change equals accomplishment toward the goal. Success in the kingdom of God is always in our reach. We just have to bring it forth in our individual lives.

I am not a television nut. It's far from my agenda most of the time. Occasionally I enjoy home improvement and organizational shows. I meditated on the shows that I watched and one day it really helped me through a stressful situation. Somebody in my household would always ask this question. "Have you seen my keys?" A long time ago I got tired of looking for my keys, so I decided that it's was time to stop wasting God's time in my life and causing myself unnecessary stress. I put my keys in one place. My rule is if you use my keys put them back in my place otherwise you will not use them again. Now, if I can get that other person in our house to do that, I won't have to say "ask the Holy Spirit," He will show you. Order is a part of our walk.

1 Corinthians 14:40 says, *"let all things be done decently and in order."*

Organization is a God thing too. We must care about how we live in everything. Here are a few tips:

- If you want to improve something develop a good habit for it. It takes time to develop a bad habit so it will take time to develop good ones too.
- Assign a place for everything.
- Use the put back method. Put things back in the right place.
- Get everybody in the household involved. These are skills that will take you over in job situations and other areas.

God's woman keeps the Word working by doing things decent and in order. She's a person of dignity. I will never forget, I was probably in my twenties then; a dynamic well known woman of God was one of the speakers at a local church. The host pastor held an intimate session with just the ladies. She spoke to us unequivocally. She made an impact in my life in that session that pushed me up a notch. It was personal dignity. I like elegant girly stuff. She talked about a lot things. And she did so candidly. You know it helps when we can be candid Honesty can bring us to our best in all things. So here I am like Paul said, "follow my example as I follow Christ." I am going to be bold and frank on personal dignity tips like that Minister was. I want to be a good example:

- Remember you are a queen.

I remember another time that another woman of God saw me on a day I was really having a terrible hair day and it was on, like my grandsons say, "church day." With the motto of "no more excuses," I had to go. One bold person, made a comment that was not pleasing to me at all but it made an irremovable mark in my life for the good, though it was not one I needed to hear, I thought. You see, if I wear sneakers, people notice and say interesting things to me. But on that occasion her comment spoke something I needed to give spiritual attention to. How we carry ourselves means something valuable to others,

> *"In everything set them an example by doing what is good"*
> **Titus2:7 NIV**

She knew my younger daughter, is a cosmetologist. Needless to say, I have no excuse. I can laugh at that now, but then I really wanted to exit the sanctuary. I just couldn't find a way out without anyone noticing. At the end of service, I rushed through the crowd to my vehicle.

- Take care of your hair.
- Get rid of the tattered under garments and the hose with runs. (It's drawer clutter) Of course nobody knows except you--and your dignity. If you are single, don't even keep them for that special time.
- Maintain good hygiene.
- Around the house; look nice. No more worn out bum clothes-- Queen.
- In keeping your house clean and organized, add this; Get rid of the faded sheets. You get the picture; it gives a perception of who you are.

This is a book in itself. Usher in your new era by giving divine attention to your domestic and personal duties. You owe it to yourself. Messy is a problem; so woman-to-God's woman, together let's get rid of THINGS wherever they are in our lives that misrepresent God's Woman. No more trying, it will never happen until we do it!

Another Life Lesson For Me

"In Him
In total submission
I am God's woman"

SHD

Intimate Moments: Time to Journal

_____
_____
_____
_____
_____
_____
_____
_____
_____
_____
_____
_____
_____
_____
_____
_____
_____
_____
_____
_____
_____

God's Woman Reaches Her Destiny

I'm not afraid to dream and I'm not afraid God won't fulfill the dreams because they came from Him. Yielding, wholeheartedly, unto Him places me in position for manifested blessings. I have always felt a specific destiny. God gives each of us a purposed life divinely connected to Him. He's given us specific gifts and talents we use for His kingdom unto His glory. It is our responsibility to seek the face of God to recognize who we are. When we discover ourselves, He will reveal your purpose to pursue.

Do you have a dream? If so, examine it. Is it God inspired and purposed?

The gifts and talents that God placed on the inside of us can be recognized and used early in life. As mothers we should look for those special traits in our children and nurture them. As wives we support them in our spouse. As women we should not lose ourselves in our roles; we connect to God, we find ourselves, our own purpose and pursue to fulfill our own destiny. One sistah' to another, we cheer one another on whether we have found or achieving our very own dreams yet or not.

I encourage you, your dreams will live, but you must provide the right fuel. Sometimes life happens it seems, and you wake up realizing that something has changed. Sometimes those unexpected changes have difficult baggage, but at that given moment you have to recognize it and do something about it.

I had a health challenge twice in my life and each time I remembered something vitally important that was going to determine whether I would win or lose the battle. I realized that the challenge was not mine and the luggage was not either. Imagine traveling and once you get to your destination you pick up your luggage and check in your hotel, as you prepare yourself for the evening you open your luggage and the contents are not yours. To your surprise you don't have anything you packed. All you know is you want your stuff back. Obviously there was another person with matching luggage, otherwise, you would have noticed before now. Well, now that you think about it, the bag did seem a little lighter than what you packed. But you picked it up and kept going. Not giving attention to slight change.

Sometimes when illnesses attack our body we may not know right away. But it is our responsibility to give ourselves what is healthy and keep the word going over ourselves everyday. So when illness came I recognized the situation. It was something to get me off focus, doubt God, and give up. You see God has already said I will live and not die. Through it all, I had the best doctors, surgeons, technicians and family and friends by my side. It was hard doing that time and at the same time I had a thorn in the flesh buffeting me everyday. The devil may use people and things to get to you, but you have to know who you are and what your purpose is. You have to give your best even when you feel like every thing is going against you and trust God. One thing about me is I'm just not a quitter. You just can't allow things or people to stand in your way no matter how tought things get. You will get those unexpected achievements and succeed by the favor of God and the faith you have and proclaimed in him. I am my Father's child and He always takes care of me. How did my challenges come out? I won and I'm still winning and fulfilling destiny, mine.

Now let me give you a Biblical example of what I'm saying to bring it home to you.

Mark 5 (NIV)

21 When Jesus had again crossed over by boat to the other side of the lake, a large crowd gathered around him while he was by the lake. 22Then one of the synagogue rulers, named Jairus, came there. Seeing Jesus, he fell at his feet 23and pleaded earnestly with him, "My little daughter is dying. Please come and put your hands on her so that she will be healed and live." 24So Jesus went with him. A large crowd followed and pressed around him. 25And a woman was there who had been subject to bleeding for twelve years. 26She had suffered a great deal under the care of many doctors and had spent all she had, yet instead of getting better she grew worse. 27When she heard about Jesus, she came up behind him in the crowd and touched his cloak, 28because she thought, "If I just touch his clothes, I will be healed." 29Immediately her bleeding stopped and she felt in her body that she was freed from her suffering. 30At once Jesus realized that power had gone out from him. He turned around in the crowd and asked, "Who touched my clothes?" 31"You see the people crowding against you," his disciples answered, "and yet you can ask, 'Who touched me?'" 32But Jesus kept looking around to see who had done it. 33Then the woman, knowing what had happened to her, came and fell at his feet and, trembling with fear, told him the whole truth. 34He said to her, "Daughter, your faith has healed you. Go in peace and be freed from your suffering."

So here we have a woman that had a dream. It took her 12 years, but she got what she dreamed for "healing." Time and money were both invested but what she did above that which caused it to come to pass was, she released her faith. She did not give up. She saw herself healed. She had passion and vision.

When you come to know and trust God nothing becomes impossible for you through Him.

Here are some things to help you as you pursue your dreams:

1. Keep your dream before your eyes, that's "vision." Write them down.
2. Fuel your dreams with the right words, action and people. Embrace and surround yourself with wholesome others that believe like you believe. Right associations will help you. Proverbs 13: 20 tell us when we *"walk with the wise"* we will in turn be what? *"Wise"* it also tells us that being *"a companion to fools"* will do what? *"Destroy you"*. Take a coffee break and Selah, on that (think on that). An important thing to remember about dreams is, share them on faithful grounds with the right friends and associates. I encourage you to examine your friendships and association list and be willing to adjust whatever is necessary to fulfill your God given purpose in life.
3. Invest in another's dream.
4. Free your self from all unforgiveness. Read Mark 11:24-26; 2 Corinthians
5. Faith is a choice, choose to believe and increase it through praying in the Holy Spirit. Jude verse 20 says, *"But you, dear friends, build yourselves up in your most holy faith and pray in the Holy Spirit."*

Trust God in it all and see yourself as God's woman who reaches her destiny.

Read "Crazy Faith" in my book *Creation's Path--A Poetic Journey of Faith*. It will encourage your faith.

Let Go Of The Past

Finally Sisters God's Woman will let go of the past.

There are those of you that have been hurt in relationships of some kind, but God wants us to let go of the past.

Your mind is a powerful part of the body. It's the place that Satan desires to take control and if he does he will destroy you. Even as I am writing God's Woman I have to keep control of my mind because he desires to stop the success of my destiny as well as helping others to forget their past. It is not always that our past is so bad, but it is the bad parts of it that the enemy tries to control.

Yes, I really believe for the impossible! So, my imagination is big! I have learned that life will move in the direction your dominating thought life, so I have decided to make it godly, good and big.

Ladies we are designers; so it is time to renew our minds so that our lives transform as God designed it from the beginning, great. For all the pain or the negative things that have held you back it's time to let it go, spring forth to the real life, yours.

Philippians and Isaiah gave us the word on that!

Philippians 3:13-14

Brethren, I do not count myself to have apprehended; but one thing I do, forgetting those things which are behind and reaching forward to those things which are ahead, I press toward the goal for the prize of the upward call of God in Christ Jesus.

Isaiah 43:18, 19

Do not remember the former things, Nor consider the
things of old.
Behold, I will do a new thing,
Now it shall spring forth;
Shall you not know it?
I will even make a road in the wilderness
And rivers in the desert

Joseph's life was another example of how to hold on to the dreams against all oppositions. Joseph was a dreamer, he had big dreams and he also had people around him that could not conceive his dreams, but rather rose up to destroy the dreamer not aware that he would be the one God used to take them from destruction to destiny.

WOW! Now say it backwards WOW! Children are like that too! They could be your Josephs. Never count a family too large even in today's times and never underestimate the potential of any of your children. They are all meant to be a blessing in their in their own designed purpose. Woe! That was truly a Holy Spirit side bar. Read the story of Joseph's life. The key point I want to make here is Joseph refused to nurture the seed of unforgiveness and hostility. He refused to doubt when others sought to destroy him. He kept on believing God. Above that he walked in love.

God's Woman

Being a woman means being your best in all the roles that we have. God made us unique and gave each of us a destiny to fulfill. We have no need to compare ourselves or our gifts and talents to another. We have our own. God desires us to fulfill our own purpose in love and support toward one another. As women we must learn to celebrate who we are as one, God's Woman.

As this desire has been in my heart over the years I have learned that being God's woman is who God created me to be and becoming her is a process that takes living one day at a time, totally and wholeheartedly unto the Lord. It's not being perfect but striving day by day for perfection; which is doing better at whatever area that God is perfecting in you right now wife, mother, sister, daughter, friend, career person and etc. God's Woman is like the saying, "I'm not getting older. I'm getting better." Go ahead and yield yourself totally to Him.

Let the Queen be seen from the inside out. You are God's Woman!

Poetic Meditations
Part 5

Divinely Packaged

Woman,
You Are
Unique, extraordinary, rare,
Extra special,
Phenomenal
Divinely created with your own purpose
Divinely packaged
Your own destiny
You are
A Queen,
A member of a royal house.

You exist in Him
You keep Him first.
You never stop growing
You never stop listening to Him
Full of wisdom
You never get too old,
Divinely packaged
You get better.

You are
Woman and wife
Pleasing to your mate,
Pleasing God
Mother, sister and grandma too.
Walking in love in all you do.
You have confidence
You are authentic
You love life and know how to celebrate each day
You are granted.

You Dream
You are a product of your Heavenly Father
Trusting in Him,
You make things happen,
Because you are destined and know it.
Nothing stops you,
Unbelief deleted by truth and faith
He trusts you in being God's woman.

The Confessions Of God's Woman

I am God's Woman
I am created in His Image
No man validates who I am
Nor in whom I belong
For I am His

In Him I move and have my being
I am God's Woman
I walk in the authority of His Word
Filled with His Spirit
I trust in Him with all my heart,
soul and might
I lean not to my own understanding
I acknowledge Him in all
He leads me down the paths in
which He has predestined for me
I am confident and
I boldly confess His word in every
situation
I am confident in who I am in Him
I am fully aware that I am nothing
without Him
And without love

I am not above my sisters or my
brothers
We are connected and one in Him
I am submissive to His will
I am God's Woman
I am the head and not the tail
I am the above and not the beneath

Blessed when I come in and when
I go out
I am His child

Daily I sit at my Heavenly Father's feet
And take heed to His instructions.
My desire is to please Him
I exercise my faith and
He manifests His Word in my
life
Riches are in my house
What I put my hands to is
blessed
The fruit of my womb is
blessed

There is none like Him
I worship Him alone
I love Him, therefore; I must
obey Him
I adorn myself inwardly with
His Word
So that He can be seen outwardly
I pray, let His will be done
through me
In total submission
I am God's woman.

Enjoy Life! Even Simple Pleasures!

Now let's enjoy the simple pleasures. God wants us to enjoy life. Finally, at some point in life I decided for myself to enjoy life, why not, we only get one on earth. You have to decide for yourself at some point, it's time to let go and let God. Let God really lead the way by His Spirit. Let God have all the cares and trust Him, it begins there anyway.

For me, when I started to relax and let God have his way I found myself enjoying the simple pleasures of a day. I started to really take time to pamper me for instance, I am not an outdoor person (I love outside scenic beauty from the inside) but since I have learned to rest in my Father's care, some days I find myself sitting out in the yard swinging or just taking a pleasure walk observing the creation. That's a miracle. I actually sat out one day for two hours. I broke a record, my own. The point I am making is what God said in Genesis one and two.

Gen 1: 31 *God looked over everything he had made; it was so good, so very good!*

I believe he took pleasure in creation.

It was evening; it was morning--Day Six.

Genesis 2 (MSG)
1 *Heaven and Earth were finished, down to the last detail.*
2-4 *By the seventh day*
God had finished his work.
On the seventh day
he rested from all his work.
God blessed the seventh day.
He made it a Holy Day
Because on that day he rested from his work,
all the creating God had done.

He took time to enjoy His creations. He rested from work. Why would God have this information in His Word? Being all-powerful God and Father, He is also an example to us. Enjoying life is what He wants for us no doubt.

Now lets end with time around the some very uplifting, reassuring scriptures through out the book of Ephesians:

Ephesians 1

Greeting
1 Paul, an apostle of Jesus Christ by the will of God, To the saints who are in Ephesus, and faithful in Christ Jesus:
2 Grace to you and peace from God our Father and the Lord Jesus Christ.

Redemption in Christ
3 Blessed be the God and Father of our Lord Jesus Christ, who has blessed us with every spiritual blessing in the heavenly places in Christ, 4 just as He chose us in Him before the foundation of the world, that we should be holy and without blame before Him in love, 5 having predestined us to adoption as sons by Jesus Christ to Himself, according to the good pleasure of His will, 6 to the praise of the glory of His grace, by which He made us accepted in the Beloved.
7 In Him we have redemption through His blood, the forgiveness of sins, according to the riches of His grace 8 which He made to abound toward us in all wisdom and prudence, 9 having made known to us the mystery of His will, according to His good pleasure which He purposed in Himself, 10 that in the dispensation of the fullness of the times He might gather together in one all things in Christ, both which are in heaven and which are on earth—in Him. 11 In Him also we have obtained an inheritance, being predestined according to the purpose of Him who works all things according to the counsel of His will, 12 that we who first trusted in Christ should be to the praise of His glory.
13 In Him you also trusted, after you heard the word of truth, the gospel of your salvation; in whom also, having believed, you were sealed with the Holy Spirit of promise, 14 who is the guarantee of our inheritance until the redemption of the purchased possession, to the praise of His glory.

Prayer for Spiritual Wisdom
15 Therefore I also, after I heard of your faith in the Lord Jesus and your love for all the saints, 16 do not cease to give thanks for you, making mention of you in my prayers: 17 that the God of our Lord Jesus Christ, the

Father of glory, may give to you the spirit of wisdom and revelation in the knowledge of Him, 18 the eyes of your understanding[c] being enlightened; that you may know what is the hope of His calling, what are the riches of the glory of His inheritance in the saints, 19 and what is the exceeding greatness of His power toward us who believe, according to the working of His mighty power 20 which He worked in Christ when He raised Him from the dead and seated Him at His right hand in the heavenly places, 21 far above all principality and power and might and dominion, and every name that is named, not only in this age but also in that which is to come. 22 And He put all things under His feet, and gave Him to be head over all things to the church, 23 which is His body, the fullness of Him who fills all in all.

Ephesians 2

By Grace Through Faith
1 And you He made alive, who were dead in trespasses and sins, 2 in which you once walked according to the course of this world, according to the prince of the power of the air, the spirit who now works in the sons of disobedience, 3 among whom also we all once conducted ourselves in the lusts of our flesh, fulfilling the desires of the flesh and of the mind, and were by nature children of wrath, just as the others. 4 But God, who is rich in mercy, because of His great love with which He loved us, 5 even when we were dead in trespasses, made us alive together with Christ (by grace you have been saved), 6 and raised us up together, and made us sit together in the heavenly places in Christ Jesus, 7 that in the ages to come He might show the exceeding riches of His grace in His kindness toward us in Christ Jesus. 8 For by grace you have been saved through faith, and that not of yourselves; it is the gift of God, 9 not of works, lest anyone should boast. 10 For we are His workmanship, created in Christ Jesus for good works, which God prepared beforehand that we should walk in them.

Brought Near by His Blood
11 Therefore remember that you, once Gentiles in the flesh—who are called Uncircumcision by what is called the Circumcision made in the flesh by hands— 12 that at that time you were without Christ, being aliens from the commonwealth of Israel and strangers from the covenants of promise, having no hope and without God in the world. 13 But now in Christ Jesus you who once were far off have been brought near by the blood of Christ.

Christ Our Peace

14 For He Himself is our peace, who has made both one, and has broken down the middle wall of separation, 15 having abolished in His flesh the enmity, that is, the law of commandments contained in ordinances, so as to create in Himself one new man from the two, thus making peace, 16 and that He might reconcile them both to God in one body through the cross, thereby putting to death the enmity. 17 And He came and preached peace to you who were afar off and to those who were near. 18 For through Him we both have access by one Spirit to the Father.

Christ Our Cornerstone

19 Now, therefore, you are no longer strangers and foreigners, but fellow citizens with the saints and members of the household of God, 20 having been built on the foundation of the apostles and prophets, Jesus Christ Himself being the chief cornerstone, 21 in whom the whole building, being fitted together, grows into a holy temple in the Lord, 22 in whom you also are being built together for a dwelling place of God in the Spirit.

Ephesians 3

The Mystery Revealed

1 For this reason I, Paul, the prisoner of Christ Jesus for you Gentiles— 2 if indeed you have heard of the dispensation of the grace of God which was given to me for you, 3 how that by revelation He made known to me the mystery (as I have briefly written already, 4 by which, when you read, you may understand my knowledge in the mystery of Christ), 5 which in other ages was not made known to the sons of men, as it has now been revealed by the Spirit to His holy apostles and prophets: 6 that the Gentiles should be fellow heirs, of the same body, and partakers of His promise in Christ through the gospel, 7 of which I became a minister according to the gift of the grace of God given to me by the effective working of His power.

Purpose of the Mystery

8 To me, who am less than the least of all the saints, this grace was given, that I should preach among the Gentiles the unsearchable riches of Christ, 9 and to make all see what is the fellowship of the mystery, which from the beginning of the ages has been hidden in God who created all things through Jesus Christ; 10 to the intent that now the manifold wisdom of God might be made known by the church to the principalities and powers in the heavenly places, 11 according to the eternal purpose which He accom-

plished in Christ Jesus our Lord, 12 in whom we have boldness and access with confidence through faith in Him. 13 Therefore I ask that you do not lose heart at my tribulations for you, which is your glory.

Appreciation of the Mystery

14 For this reason I bow my knees to the Father of our Lord Jesus Christ, 15 from whom the whole family in heaven and earth is named, 16 that He would grant you, according to the riches of His glory, to be strengthened with might through His Spirit in the inner man, 17 that Christ may dwell in your hearts through faith; that you, being rooted and grounded in love, 18 may be able to comprehend with all the saints what is the width and length and depth and height— 19 to know the love of Christ which passes knowledge; that you may be filled with all the fullness of God.

20 Now to Him who is able to do exceedingly abundantly above all that we ask or think, according to the power that works in us, 21 to Him be glory in the church by Christ Jesus to all generations, forever and ever. Amen

Ephesians 4

Walk in Unity

1 I, therefore, the prisoner of the Lord, beseech you to walk worthy of the calling with which you were called, 2 with all lowliness and gentleness, with longsuffering, bearing with one another in love, 3 endeavoring to keep the unity of the Spirit in the bond of peace. 4 There is one body and one Spirit, just as you were called in one hope of your calling; 5 one Lord, one faith, one baptism; 6 one God and Father of all, who is above all, and through all, and in you all.

Spiritual Gifts

7 But to each one of us grace was given according to the measure of Christ's gift. 8 Therefore He says: When He ascended on high, He led captivity captive, And gave gifts to men. 9 (Now this, "He ascended"—what does it mean but that He also first descended into the lower parts of the earth? 10 He who descended is also the One who ascended far above all the heavens, that He might fill all things.) 11 And He Himself gave some to be apostles, some prophets, some evangelists, and some pastors and teachers, 12 for the equipping of the saints for the work of ministry, for the edifying of the body of Christ, 13 till we all come to the unity of the faith and of the knowledge of the Son of God, to a perfect man, to the measure of the stature of the fullness of Christ; 14 that we should no longer be children, tossed to and

fro and carried about with every wind of doctrine, by the trickery of men, in the cunning craftiness of deceitful plotting, 15 but, speaking the truth in love, may grow up in all things into Him who is the head—Christ— 16 from whom the whole body, joined and knit together by what every joint supplies, according to the effective working by which every part does its share, causes growth of the body for the edifying of itself in love.

The New Man

17 This I say, therefore, and testify in the Lord, that you should no longer walk as the rest of the Gentiles walk, in the futility of their mind, 18 having their understanding darkened, being alienated from the life of God, because of the ignorance that is in them, because of the blindness of their heart; 19 who, being past feeling, have given themselves over to lewdness, to work all uncleanness with greediness.

20 But you have not so learned Christ, 21 if indeed you have heard Him and have been taught by Him, as the truth is in Jesus: 22 that you put off, concerning your former conduct, the old man which grows corrupt according to the deceitful lusts, 23 and be renewed in the spirit of your mind, 24 and that you put on the new man which was created according to God, in true righteousness and holiness.

Do Not Grieve the Spirit

25 Therefore, putting away lying, " Let each one of you speak truth with his neighbor, for we are members of one another. 26 "Be angry, and do not sin" :do not let the sun go down on your wrath, 27 nor give place to the devil. 28 Let him who stole steal no longer, but rather let him labor, working with his hands what is good, that he may have something to give him who has need. 29 Let no corrupt word proceed out of your mouth, but what is good for necessary edification, that it may impart grace to the hearers. 30 And do not grieve the Holy Spirit of God, by whom you were sealed for the day of redemption. 31 Let all bitterness, wrath, anger, clamor, and evil speaking be put away from you, with all malice. 32 And be kind to one another, tenderhearted, forgiving one another, even as God in Christ forgave you.

Ephesians 5

Walk in Love

1 Therefore be imitators of God as dear children. 2 And walk in love, as Christ also has loved us and given Himself for us, an offering and a sacri-

fice to God for a sweet-smelling aroma. 3 But fornication and all uncleanness or covetousness, let it not even be named among you, as is fitting for saints; 4 neither filthiness, nor foolish talking, nor coarse jesting, which are not fitting, but rather giving of thanks. 5 For this you know, that no fornicator, unclean person, nor covetous man, who is an idolater, has any inheritance in the kingdom of Christ and God. 6 Let no one deceive you with empty words, for because of these things the wrath of God comes upon the sons of disobedience. 7 Therefore do not be partakers with them.

Walk in Light

8 For you were once darkness, but now you are light in the Lord. Walk as children of light 9 (for the fruit of the Spirit is in all goodness, righteousness, and truth), 10 finding out what is acceptable to the Lord. 11 And have no fellowship with the unfruitful works of darkness, but rather expose them. 12 For it is shameful even to speak of those things which are done by them in secret. 13 But all things that are exposed are made manifest by the light, for whatever makes manifest is light. 14 Therefore He says: Awake, you who sleep, Arise from the dead, And Christ will give you light.

Walk in Wisdom

15 See then that you walk circumspectly, not as fools but as wise, 16 redeeming the time, because the days are evil.
17 Therefore do not be unwise, but understand what the will of the Lord is. 18 And do not be drunk with wine, in which is dissipation; but be filled with the Spirit, 19 speaking to one another in psalms and hymns and spiritual songs, singing and making melody in your heart to the Lord, 20 giving thanks always for all things to God the Father in the name of our Lord Jesus Christ, 21 submitting to one another in the fear of God.

Please continue your reading in Ephesians 5:22-31, 6:1-19 from your Bible you will be blessed as God speaks to your heart. I pray that he gives you a new revelation of your walk as God's woman. v. 20…That in it I may speak boldly, as I ought to speak. Faithful minister in the Lord, will make all things known to you; 22 whom I have sent to you for this very purpose, that you may know our affairs, and that he may comfort your hearts. 23 Peace to the brethren, and love with faith, from God the Father and the Lord Jesus Christ. 24 Grace be with all those who love our Lord Jesus Christ in sincerity. Amen.

I end with this book of Ephesians because it appropriately expresses the bank account we have in the kingdom of God as his sons and daughters through Jesus Christ and sealed by the Holy Spirit. When we draw this huge endowment, we see that we have all the resources needed for living in the love, peace, joy and provisions of God. We also see we have all the resources to be God's Woman.   Amen.

About The Author

Photo - Lacy Smith

Sharon D. Stevenson Holliday

is an inspiring anointed woman of God. She is a woman of the Word that loves God very much. She is a woman that has worn many hats personally and professionally.

She is a minister of the Word of God along with her husband Minister Ransom D. Holliday. As the pioneer of her local church's children and youth ministry she has dedicated 15 years of ministry in its development and spiritual growth for children, teens, parents, and leadership.

She and her husband have two adult daughters, Monica & Sherisa, one adult son Tyshon, one son and daughter in-law Qunicey and Akiah, four grandsons: L'Isaiah, Quincey Jr., Steven, and Tyshon Jr.

She is a published author, poet, and greeting card writer. God blessed her with a gift to be an inspiration to many.

She admires the strength of her mother, Esther Thomas and the special love that she has given her that spurs her to be strong in the Lord and to be God's Woman. She's always encouraged by her father's (James Moore Sr.) love. Sharon prays that her life somehow adds to their lives, her Heavenly Father's Joy.

God's Woman *In Her Own Destiny*

Order Form

Please print clearly

Please send me _____ copies of *God's Woman* by Sharon D. Holliday

Name _____

Company (if applicable)_____

City _____ State _____ Zip _____

Day phone _____ Evening _____

E-mail _____

Cost: **$12.⁰⁰**

Quantity of books	$_____
Subtotal	$_____
Sales Tax	
NC Residents add 7%	$_____
Shipping & Handling	$_____
	$_____
Total	$_____

Please send this coupon and you check or money order to:

Sharon Holliday
P.O. Box 13093
Durham, NC 27709   Payable to: **Sharon Holliday**

Online ordering log on to: *www.sharonholliday.org*

I Will Go As He Desires...

Book Sharon for reading, ministry, women conference and other engagements contact by email: *poet@sharonholliday.org* or *sharondholliday@yahoo.com*

Thank you for your order. God bless you!